PORTRAITS DESTROYED

First published in Australia in 2019
by Thames & Hudson Australia Pty Ltd
11 Central Boulevard, Portside Business Park
Port Melbourne, Victoria 3207
ABN: 72 004 751 964

www.thamesandhudson.com.au

Thames & Hudson Australia wishes to acknowledge that Aboriginal and Torres Strait Islander people are the first storytellers of this nation and the traditional custodians of the land on which we live and work. We acknowledge their continuing culture and pay respect to Elders past, present and future.

978 1 7607600 6 9

 A catalogue record for this
book is available from the
NATIONAL LIBRARY OF AUSTRALIA
National Library of Australia

Every effort has been made to trace accurate ownership of copyrighted text and visual materials used in this book. Errors or omissions will be corrected in subsequent editions, provided notification is sent to the publisher.

Jacket front: Graham Sutherland (1903–1980), *Winston Churchill*, 1954
Jacket back: Mao Zedong portrait on Gate of Heavenly Peace, Tiananmen Square, Beijing, 2012, photograph. Image: Gavin Hellier/Alamy Stock Photo
Front flap: *Captain Cook Statue Vandalised*, 25 January 2018, photograph. Image: Nicole Garmston
Back flap: *Bronze Portrait Bust of a Roman Matron (Agrippina)*, c.20–50 CE
Cover and text design: John Canty
Typesetting: Megan Ellis
Editing: Vanessa Battersby
Printed and bound in Malaysia by Times Offset (M) Sdn Bhd

PORTRAITS DESTROYED

Power, ego and history's vandals

JULIE COTTER

Thames & Hudson

CONTENTS

INTRODUCTION

Bells rang the alarm at midnight as the Catholic court headed to Christmas Eve mass. Madrid's royal palace, the Alcázar, was on fire. It was 1734.

The bells were initially ignored, such was the urgency to satisfy religious obligations, but when volumes of smoke began to fill the vast rooms and hallways, court officials, monks and servants set in motion a rescue. If not for their passion, their sense of duty and their belief in the importance of the portrait to the court – and, indeed, to the Spanish people – the supreme work by Spanish Golden Age master Diego Velázquez, *Las Meninas* (1656; Museo del Prado, Madrid) [Figure 1], would be known only from copies and descriptions. Over three metres tall and almost three metres wide, the painting was torn from its frame and thrown out the window to its fate below. Chests full of gold and precious jewels including the famed Peregrina pearl were hauled from their places of safe-keeping and cast over balconies. Other paintings were also rescued but, in total, the fire destroyed at least five hundred artworks from King Philip V's collection of over two thousand pieces, and reduced the Alcázar to rubble.

Las Meninas is an extraordinary, carefully constructed work of seventeenth-century realism, testifying to the grand age of Spanish court life and the cosseted existence of the Infanta Margarita Teresa, shown surrounded by family and attendants. One of only five of Philip IV's fourteen (legitimate) children to live beyond childhood, the Infanta would become, by marriage, the Holy Roman Empress and German Queen – among other titles – before her death at the age of twenty-one. (As an indication of the consanguinity of the Spanish court, she married an uncle who was also her paternal cousin: perhaps unsurprisingly, from her six pregnancies, only four children were born alive and only one lived beyond infancy.) Today, the picture is missing edges that were swallowed by the fire, but, incredibly, a mark on the cheek of the young Infanta was the only real damage to the body of the work.

The scene for *Las Meninas* is the withering Alcázar itself – not Velázquez's studio, but a room he had hunted through the palace to find. The light had to sweep through the darkened spaces and allow room for the tableau arrangement of royal subjects, while works by Rubens line the high walls in homage to the other artist. And just as the room is filled with the content of his friend and colleague, so too is the space filled with ourselves, by virtue of the mirror in which we see the Infanta's parents, King Philip IV and Queen Mariana of Austria, reflected as though they stand beside us. The Infanta and her maids and assistants gaze at us – or do they look at the royal parents who have suddenly appeared to observe the painting of the portrait? Hovering with his brush in hand is the splendidly attired Velázquez in court fashion, the high collar supporting the haughty look he casts as though he were royalty.

Velázquez has painted himself standing before a large canvas, his current work, the back of the canvas painted into the side of

Las Meninas. His work is a study of disorder at a time of strict royal protocol and standards, the corseted young Infanta testimony to such protocol. The structure, the gaze and the characters of *Las Meninas* have inspired writers, painters and casual observers for centuries. Sir Thomas Lawrence, the pre-eminent European portrait painter of the late eighteenth and early nineteenth centuries, called the work 'the true philosophy of art'.

I had been warned, via the writings of Sir Kenneth Clark, Michel Foucault and Jacques Lacan (among others), that upon standing in front of this work I would feel as though I were an intrinsic part of it. Nevertheless, it was quite a jolt that first time in the early evening at the Museo del Prado. Here before me was the iconic picture to which artists such as Manet, Whistler, Sargent, Chase, Picasso and Dalí had made pilgrimages. They stood before the work (although Whistler didn't quite make it and remained content with a copy), marvelled at the luminous spaces, had to adjust their eyes to the detail in the dark voids and then return to meet the gaze of Velázquez – he does not allow the hapless viewer to peel away too easily.

I stood in front of the painting every day of that visit to Madrid. Picasso maintained the originality of his work, yet he returned time and again to stand before *Las Meninas*, to contemplate the structure, the gazes from within, and produced a substantial body of work in the process. I wondered at the staging of the figures, contemplated the lines of sight Foucault had identified, and pondered the swirling, gaping sinkhole that would have existed in art practice if this painting had been destroyed. It's like contemplating your existence with one forebear missing – you could not, in theory, have been born.

Without its puzzles of time and space, of Velázquez's unwavering commitment to his subject, of the intimacy of a scene that equally is the most momentous, what would contemporary art practice look like?

In time, our age will be referred to as the age of the portrait. People in the future will wonder at our obsession with self, and with the celebrities who 'selflessly' post pictures from every angle. My children have pictures of every friend and relative they've ever had, of every nuance of every event – and via social media, they can see every friend their friends have. They're blissfully unfamiliar with the concept of waiting for a roll of film to be developed, hoping for perfect pictures – let alone waiting for a painstakingly painted portrait to be completed over weeks or months. Egalitarian, intimate and instantaneous, social media has made the portrait a defining element in our society. And today, a portrait may be destroyed as quickly as it is registered.

Artists often dispose of painted portraits of themselves, their friends and their commissions as part of the creative process. When Charles Edmund Brock was commissioned in 1936 to paint the group portrait of the Queen Mother and her daughters Princess Elizabeth and Princess Margaret, he completed eight versions. One went to Buckingham Palace, one he kept and the other six paintings were destroyed. It's natural for an artist to cull works he or she considers unsuccessful.

The legacy of Frida Kahlo's work is significantly reduced due to many of her 270 known pieces being lost, destroyed or possibly in unknown collections. Kahlo expert Helga Prignitz-Poda has identified at least twenty-six lost works.[1] Kahlo destroyed some of her early experimental portraits, as artists often do, but with the development of her work came a realisation of its impact and relevance. Kahlo chose as the subject of one of her beautiful, pensive portraits the model and muse Lupe Marin, the second wife of Diego Rivera; he ultimately became Kahlo's husband in 1929.

Marin and Kahlo became friends, prompting Kahlo, enamoured with her beauty, to paint Marin's portrait in 1929. Unfortunately, Marin, known for destroying Rivera's work during fits of jealousy, destroyed Kahlo's portrait with a pair of scissors following a quarrel. Their relationship remained volatile, and Kahlo's second marriage to Rivera caused Marin further anguish. Kahlo, in anger, wrote to a friend that 'everything that she does is so low and dirty that sometimes I feel like going back to Mexico and kill her'.[2] Much later, and confined to bed in inexorable pain, Kahlo destroyed a 1954 self-portrait that she felt portrayed her with an energy she no longer possessed. Just as Kahlo's body of work is inextricably linked to her personal life, so is the destruction of her work.

Nevertheless, artists do not usually destroy a commissioned and carefully constructed portrayal, nor do they expect their subjects to do so. When Graham Sutherland was told of the destruction of his portrait of Prime Minister Winston Churchill, he responded that he considered it an act of unwarranted vandalism. Yet he knew Churchill hated the portrait and that pleasing him was never going to be a simple task. It's difficult dealing with reputations, desire, allure and history. A portrait often binds all of these characteristics together through the eyes of a single artist.

The fate of two portraits by Australian artist Lewis Miller of former Prime Minister Malcolm Turnbull and his wife, Lucy, remains murky. In 1992 Miller was commissioned to paint a double portrait of the power couple and travelled to their farm in the Hunter Valley in New South Wales to sketch them. All that appears to remain of this enterprise are those few sketches. Miller painted the Turnbull portraits in profile, in the style of Renaissance artist Piero della Francesca. The painted portraits were duly delivered but never seen again, Malcolm and Lucy apparently not at all happy with the result. Miller worked up his sketches from the Hunter Valley trip to produce a further portrait for the Archibald Prize but took to that with a craft knife, destroying the work.[3]

The destruction, damage or theft of a painted or carefully photographed portrait remains an act of shocking violence – as though the very person were attacked. For good or otherwise, the portrait stands in for the one represented; when artist Basil Hallward waves a threatening knife at the portrait in Oscar Wilde's *The Picture of Dorian Gray*, Gray pulls the knife out of his hand: 'Don't, Basil, don't!' he cried. 'It would be murder!' The portrait in the story becomes the living, breathing being, the murderous actions of Gray causing the portrait to darken and decay.

Of course, at times, the attack is warranted and even welcome, as with the destruction of the portraits of an overthrown dictator. The power of portraiture, its ability to engage and inspire, is intrinsic to the establishment of the power invested in one person. Portraits are repeatedly displayed within the public arena to ensure the official image permeates all work and domestic spaces: Hitler, Stalin and Zimbabwe's Robert Mugabe all benefited from the repetition of the portrait image to secure their message and their following. But power is nothing if not transient, whether bestowed through elected political leadership, military coup or revolutionary force.

There are two reasons that few portraits of Mary Queen of Scots exist. Firstly, she was too late to develop an understanding of the cult of celebrity facilitated by the portrait, and secondly, the best means of eradicating support for any person is to destroy their portrait. If King James VI of Scotland had possessed a sincere, contemporary portrait of his mother, Mary, perhaps painted in the style of the portraiture of Queen Elizabeth I, might he have tried harder to rescue her from the gallows? There were many forces in play to ensure Mary could not gain any traction with her son. Her letters were intercepted, her desire to return to Scotland left unanswered. A fine portrait risked attachment on the part of a son who had not seen his mother since he was an infant. If a captivating portrait had greeted King James VI every morning, would the course of history have been altered?

Portraits are destroyed as a means to obliterate the memory of a person; to deny someone their right to a title or heritage; to control image or legacy; out of vengeance; or to draw attention to a political or moral view. Then, of course, there are the motivations of vanity and artistic trauma.

Fire is a pervasive tyrant in this book. Burning rather than cutting up a portrait is the more usual – and quicker – remedy to ensure the act of destruction is complete – akin to burning a body and the evidence. Nothing is left to be rescued. Whether it be portraits of Queen Elizabeth I that neglected to preserve her 'mask of youth', the Churchill portrait, presidential portraits that failed to convey the stature and power of the office holder, the many depictions of Adolf

Hitler or simply the quiet, unassuming portraits by artists heralded as 'degenerate' by the Nazi regime – the lustrous bonfire was, ultimately, their destiny.

This book deliberately roams across periods of art to mine society's connections and responses to the trauma, loss and joy that can emanate from the destruction of a portrait. From the perspective of the academic to the musings of a President on social media, the intrinsic value of portraiture takes on heroic proportions. Like it or not, portraits define us as a nation and as people. The negation and interception of that narrative cuts deeply into our identity. Conversely, that destruction also has something to say about our morals, principles and vanity.

It is the portrait taken from life that is discreetly positioned as the hero in this book – its loss all the more potent. But why do we care so much? Surely the letters and diaries, the historical records and learned perspectives that often saturate the biographical space of a subject, are enough? The reason lies within the accessibility of the visual. We need portraits of a notable figure so that we may ease ourselves into a moment, an epoch or an explosion of history. The portrait can operate as a document that tells us a great deal about a person. When the subject is core to our history, destruction of a portrait is a negation of our right to know and understand our past.

CHAPTER 1

Bulldog or Cherub: The Legacy of Winston Churchill

Prime Minister Winston Churchill entered a packed Westminster Hall at noon on 10 November 1954 to the sound of drummers beating out a V in Morse code. It would have meant little to the majority of parliamentarians and dignitaries assembled, but to Churchill, the soldier, politician, writer, orator and military historian, it was a charming homage to his signature gesture. He and his wife, Clementine Churchill, had arrived to attend the unveiling of a commemorative portrait by the renowned British artist Graham Sutherland, painted to honour the eightieth birthday of a man who had served his beloved Britain for sixty years [Figure 2].

This was the second time Churchill had held the office of Prime Minister; his first period of service saw him lead Britain to a debilitating yet gallant victory in World War II. Surprise and disbelief was felt among many quarters when he was voted out of office only two months after heroically declaring 8 May 1945 as VE Day for all of Europe. He remained in opposition for six years, refused to resign to allow a younger man to take over and stood firm in his perennial belief that he had the brio to govern in spite of his advancing years. His resilience and popularity with the British people were validated when he was again elected to the Prime Ministerial position in 1951. Churchill was seventy-seven, undaunted by his advancing years and the complexity of Cold War issues.

Vanity is intrinsically linked to power; to be powerful you must be extremely confident in your abilities as well as perceptibly attractive to a public who must support you. While Churchill's cabinet held expectations that sometime in 1953 he might resign out of deference to Foreign Secretary Anthony Eden, he would later become egregiously angered by suggestions he should cease his service to the British Empire, bouts of ill health that had included a stroke in the previous year notwithstanding. The stroke had not been made public and Churchill believed he was as fit, erudite and strategic as ever. He trusted in his ability to govern above any other candidate. Yet he was not the Churchill they once knew, he often struggled to convince his colleagues and those in opposition of his intuitive leadership of old. By 1954 he was in the twilight of his career, working to arrange and edit 'the part he will play in history', as his physician Lord Moran put it.[1] He may have assumed that his friends and enemies would allow him the grace to do so: but things are rarely so simple.

On that day in November 1954, before a packed audience of Members of Parliament and distinguished guests, Opposition

Leader Clement Attlee stood at the podium on a stage that held Churchill, his wife, close colleagues and Sutherland, and asked Churchill to accept the portrait as a gift on behalf of the joint Houses of Parliament. The curtains that covered the portrait, as though it were a dedicatory plaque, were ceremoniously drawn back. Churchill stood and turned to look at the portrait as it was unveiled – he knew exactly what everyone was about to see.

Churchill had always hoped that the ceremony to mark his eightieth birthday would be one of majestic trumpets ringing in his ears and a magnificent dedication to his character and service to Empire. But he had spent a lifetime preparing himself for unrealised expectations. What he witnessed before him was the unveiling of a portrait that he believed said nothing about his service. What he heard from the audience were muffled chuckles, murmurings and sporadic clapping. There was cringing and peering over the tops of spectacles and women stealing glances at the picture from beneath the brims of their cloche hats.

Sutherland had depicted Churchill as aged, incapacitated and of dwindling stature. The heroic, demonstrative, captivating bulldog had withered to become simply a man in a striped suit slumped in a deep club chair. He appeared as though dressed for the position of Prime Minister but frailty had overwhelmed him to the point that he now lacked the strength and the will to manoeuvre his large body to perform an everyday task.

There had been considerable visual documentation of Churchill throughout his career. The younger, fitter Churchill standing to attention in military uniform, the formidable politician gruffly facing the camera or the sophisticated savant in evening dress, standing beside the petite young Queen Elizabeth, Churchill staring uncompromisingly at the camera, ready to defend Britain for his Queen and country. But a life such as that lived by Churchill is more complex than a public persona. Sutherland wanted a portrait that depicted the physical evidence of the eighty-year-old man he had encountered, drawn and engaged deeply in conversation, not the political performer. For a number of Churchill's colleagues sitting at the ceremony that day, there was no more profound pleasure than to see the great man not represented as the heroic symbol of modern Britain. Finally, he was one of them.

Ever the consummate performer, however, Churchill defused the moment masterfully in his acceptance speech. 'The portrait is a remarkable example of modern art,' he quipped, to laughter and applause from the crowd. Churchill would not be beaten by a portrait; he would leave his guests with memories of his humour, his service and his spirit [Figure 3].

The portrait would not see the light of day again. It was consigned to storage in the cellars of Chartwell Manor, and following Churchill's death some ten years later in 1965, the painting's fate was made clear: it had been burned at the behest of his wife, Clementine.

Clementine had supported and moulded Churchill's image with sophisticated flair, and the story that she personally burnt the canvas has permeated popular culture. However, a recording by Churchill's private secretary, Grace Hamblin, discovered by historian Sonia Purnell in the Churchill archives in 2015, reveals the truth.

The formerly sealed tape by Hamblin includes testimony that the size (1.47 × 1.21 metres) and weight of the canvas would have made it physically impossible for the elderly Clementine to carry it to the garden and burn it alone. The tape reveals that Hamblin – acting without instruction – asked her brother, a gardener, to assist her in moving the painting from the Chartwell cellar to his house. There, in her brother's garden, the portrait of one of the most notable people in twentieth-century history was burned.

Mary Soames, daughter of Winston and Clementine, wrote a biography of her mother and clearly enjoys the details of her mother's protection of her father's image. Mary accompanied Clementine on the day she first viewed the portrait and, intriguingly, relates that her mother's first reaction was favourable: she 'spoke of it with approval, and praised its truthfulness'. It was only later that Clementine developed a hatred of the work, no doubt influenced by Churchill's response.

Interestingly, Soames defends Clementine's right to destroy the portrait against criticism that the Churchill family did not own the portrait – that it was not their portrait to dispose of. It appears that originally the notion was to produce a portrait to hang in the House of Commons, but this was not pursued. The copyright of Sutherland's portrait was assigned to Churchill, which meant he and his family could do as they pleased. Soames also records Clementine as destroying two previous portraits of Churchill, one by the talented British artist Walter Sickert and the other by Paul Maze, a Post-Impressionist artist whom Churchill met on the Western Front.

Sickert was a longstanding friend of Churchill's and a childhood friend of Clementine's, but 'this had not deterred her from putting her foot through a sketch he had done of Winston sometime around 1927 which she disliked'.[2] It seems that this story of portrait destruction was 'casually mentioned' to Sutherland by Churchill during the painting of his portrait as a warning that his greatest critic would, in fact, be Clementine.[3]

Winston and Clementine came across the Maze portrait of Churchill during a visit to the home of Franklin D. Roosevelt in Hyde Park, New York, after the Second Quebec Conference in 1944. The picture was hanging in the President's Museum, and Clementine informed the President that she did not like it. Roosevelt replied that neither did he, upon which Clementine saw her chance:

So I said, 'May it come out?' and he said, 'Yes' and so now it is destroyed.[4]

Maze's career was certainly not harmed by the action: he would later serve as the official painter of Queen Elizabeth's coronation in 1953, having undertaken the same role at the funeral of King George VI. And Maze and Churchill maintained a lifelong friendship, often painting together and discussing art in their correspondence.

So why was Sutherland's portrait considered such a failure? Surely Churchill was the easiest of subjects. There is no greater gift for a portrait artist than a person of substantial form and character – particularly one who enjoys the performance of self, as Churchill did.

It's said that a successful portrait is a summation of a life – an exclamation mark upon all that has been achieved and is yet to be discovered. Churchill was a self-fashioned celebrity and the public had become attuned to the dissemination of a certain image of him in the pages of the newspapers and the newsreels of conspicuous parliamentary events. A portrait of the eminent leader should surely pay homage to that image. Sutherland's portrait was indeed a reflection of all Churchill had become throughout his life. The disjuncture between the final picture and the expectations of the portrait's subject and the public has three main causes.

Firstly, the choice of painter: Graham Sutherland was a highly talented British artist whose reputation had developed through his work as a war artist and images of the British landscape. He had not produced many portraits prior to the Churchill commission, with the few examples being statements of character of the subject rather than official commissions. His approach was to search avidly for the subject beneath the exterior rather than negotiate the subject's public image.

Secondly, Churchill's self-image was an entity he had spent a lifetime colonising within the pages of popular literature, war histories and autobiographies – he believed in his ability to define who he was rather than leave it to a fledgling portrait artist.

And thirdly, Churchill's public persona as a man of cigar-fuelled power overrode all else.

While Churchill's ancestry was one of privilege and entitlement, it was nobility peppered with the vagaries of exhausting wealth held in palaces – but little cash. Born at Blenheim Palace, he was the son of Lord Randolph Churchill and grandson of the seventh Duke of Marlborough. But Churchill fortuitously had an American-born mother, Jeannette 'Jennie' Jerome. The cross-Atlantic connection supported by the familial associations would later assume a world stage in Churchill's strategic alliance and firm friendship with President Franklin D. Roosevelt during World War II. Much later, the American people bestowed their thanks upon Churchill by making him an honorary citizen.

Churchill's maternal grandfather, Leonard Jerome, held some influence in America through his publishing business – he was one of the new age entrepreneurs – but stockmarket crashes and bad investments significantly decreased his wealth during Jennie's lifetime. When Lord Churchill died in 1895 at just forty-five, Jennie and her two sons, Winston and Jack, were often in debt, only periodically relieved by hurried requests for assistance from wealthy cousins. Lord Churchill's assets were placed into a trust for the boys but he left no allowance for them in the intervening period, forcing Churchill to seek employment early in life.

Eager to earn an income and to pursue a military career, Churchill obtained a position with the 4th Queen's Own Hussars in 1895 at twenty years of age. He would combine this career with activity as a war correspondent from countries as far afield as Cuba, Egypt, South Africa – where he was imprisoned but managed to escape – and India. His energy was extraordinary, engendering the jealousy of some and the admiration of others. It was a situation that changed little throughout his life.

Churchill was ambitious, sought opportunities to promote his talents and achievements and flagrantly ignored rules and procedures when it suited him. When Lieutenant Winston Churchill continued to forward dispatches from what was known as the 'River War' (the reclamation of the Sudan), he stirred the wrath of not only General Kitchener but also the Prince of Wales. His Royal Highness, perturbed by details from dispatches that found their way into the *Morning Post*, was forced to write to Churchill reminding him that it was not appropriate for a serving officer to discuss operations with the press![5]

It did not stop Churchill – not a great deal did. He believed his career could bypass any major or minor mishap, lived each day to every possible advantage and encouraged others to do the same. He even pulled up his sleeve and willingly donated a slice of his own skin to a wounded soldier who desperately needed a skin graft during the Battle of Omdurman, one of the last actions of the Sudan campaign.

His rise to the halls of Parliament could be considered meteoric: he entered politics and won the seat of Oldham in 1900, at the age of twenty-five. The prying eyes of those who sought Churchill's demise were never diverted from their warrant, while others believed in his humanity. His proclaimed support for 'the left-out millions' in 1906 befitted his newfound membership of the Liberal Party and his convictions. He had dramatically crossed the floor in 1904 to leave the Conservative Party, and later advocated for what were then radical social welfare programs.[6] With the impending war, and drawing upon his Boer War service, Churchill was assigned to the post of First Lord of the Admiralty and thereafter was placed in substantial roles of authority throughout the war. It is this service for which he is most heavily criticised; the beach landings of the ill-prepared Anzacs at Gallipoli are the subject of much debate. In defiance of the criticism, his ostracism from Parliament and what he considered the lack of use of his substantial skills, he chose to enlist and served on the Western Front in France.

Churchill, if nothing else, stood by his convictions. Hurt by the criticism, and with his brother Jack serving in the First Anzac Corps, Churchill faced his opponents both within Britain and on enemy ground. He, of course, returned after the war to continue his political career, but it was not smooth sailing. It's difficult to imagine the inner strength that must have been required, after such a demonstrative rejection on his part, for him to later re-join the Conservative Party in 1924. He became Chancellor of the Exchequer under Stanley Baldwin, but his political journey had not become easier and he dramatically exhibited an arrogance towards the miners in the tumultuous General Strike of 1926 that won him few friends.

It is from this period until World War II that Churchill enters what are commonly referred to as his wilderness years. His career continued to be typified by the expression of frank and deliberate opinions and the taking of actions independently to achieve his objectives – exasperating his colleagues, particularly those in Cabinet. It pitched him as a loner, his heavy shoulders required to carry the weight of criticism from all flanks and assume the responsibility for his decisions.

Until his marriage, Churchill relied heavily upon his mother to manage his personal affairs, including selling his manuscripts, dealing with publishers and, of course, advancing funds. His letters to her from the depths of battlefields, Parisian hotels and Parliament reveal their usual dire financial situation. Things were at such a low ebb at one stage that Churchill broached the prospect of his mother remarrying. 'I hate the idea of your marrying but that of course would be a solution,' he wrote during their negotiations to rearrange the inheritance left by his father.[7] It is a seemingly harsh response, but equally one from a man who strove to survive at all costs.

Churchill himself was encouraged to seek a 'rich heiress' as a lifelong partner, and he encountered many within his social circle. But he married for love in 1908 Clementine Hozier, the daughter of titled parents acquainted with artistic and literary circles, although she was in need of funds as much as her husband.[8] He was attracted to both her beauty and her character, her fierce protection of Churchill's reputation earning the admiration of many throughout her life.

Churchill was ever the optimist, however, believing in his ability to raise funds through his many and varied writing ventures, including biographies of his father and of John Churchill, 1st Duke of Marlborough. Indeed, his income from writing significantly outstripped his military and parliamentary salaries. However, his financial situation was as strained when he married as previously, and the births of five children added to the considerable financial burden of life's expenses – particularly given his many leisure activities.

The glamour of Churchill's war heroics was nothing compared to the glamour of his personal life and associations. When he was transferred to the front in World War I, he exulted in the opportunity to observe the French army and meet Prime Minister Clemenceau. Soon after the war finished, he commenced his real love affair with the lifestyle and beauty of the south of France. The Panorama Hotel in Cassis in the 1920s was one of his favourites. He passed many an hour of the summer months there in the company of the bejewelled, the famous and the beautiful, carousing in the homes of wealthy friends embedded in refined European society. In the dilettante set, the company of the great man was highly desired, while Clementine tended to keep her distance and remained in England.

Money, as discussed, was not something of which Churchill had an endless supply. He spent it as easily as he acquired it and was almost permanently in debt to British lending institutions or empathetic friends. He relied upon the invitations of the wealthy to fulfil his multifarious ambitions – which primarily revolved around painting in the south of France in the footsteps of his favoured French Impressionists, gambling at the casinos and writing his many books and essays in the Riviera warmth. The bitter cold of England was never his preference.

During the twenties and thirties, when Churchill's life had few political obligations, he often stayed at the luxurious Château de l'Horizon at Vallauris near Cannes, which belonged to former American actress and supreme social hostess Maxine Elliott. Churchill's day would commence with a visit from his secretary, Miss Penman, who would prop herself on the end of the bed while Churchill dictated pages of his latest book – 1500 words at a time not out of the question – and attended to his correspondence to all and sundry. He would then lunch beside the pool, prior to a contented afternoon of painting.

Following this, he would receive the product of his morning's work, beautifully prepared on carefully typed pages. Then it was off to dress for dinner and to be his entertaining best with Maxine's other house guests before, on occasion, sneaking away to the casino. His vigour must have exhausted the best of them while his work during this time continues to inform historical accounts of the period. Most significantly, however, Churchill was at his most outspoken in the thirties in his efforts to awaken the sleeping lion to meet what he considered the imminent threat of war. Neville Chamberlain was the Prime Minister, and Churchill was his most ardent critic.

Churchill was well positioned in the thirties to assess the growing unrest. He remained within earshot of the mumblings of Nazi aspirations and was fearful of what might occur, warning his colleagues of the danger looming from the alliance of Adolf Hitler and Italy's Benito Mussolini. But no one believed that war was on their doorstep. Even the Duke of Windsor (who by 1938 had abdicated and was ensconced in a rented villa at Cap d'Antibes, not far from the Château de l'Horizon) challenged Churchill's assessment of the situation.

The outbreak of war catapulted Churchill, a man agitated at his lack of power yet content with his semi-leisured 'artistic' state, to leadership of the Allied Forces. Of course, he was not brought into the fold without question: there were many attempts to destabilise his governance over the ensuing years. Churchill's response to an attempt by the Australian Prime Minister Robert Menzies to thwart his control was an extraordinary act of resilience, arrogance and self-confidence.

In 1941, Menzies challenged the authoritarian management of the war by Churchill. He had been deeply disturbed by the lack of consultation with Australia regarding the decision to move the Pacific Fleet to the Atlantic; in conversation with the likes of Conservative MP Victor Cazalet, Menzies referred to Churchill as a 'dictator'.[9] Churchill's desultory Cabinet – mostly former members of Neville Chamberlain's government who were comfortable with a far more collaborative command – quickly commissioned Menzies to challenge Churchill. Whispers in Menzies' ear proffered elevation and participation in the British governance of the war, and he was sounded out as a member of a possible war cabinet in London.

He had flown far too close to the sun. Churchill was not interested in sharing the leadership and had no regard for the ability of anyone else to lead the allies. It's a striking demonstration of Churchill's strength of character – a strength he strove to convey, not only in the company of his colleagues, but also through the many portraits for which he was a most sought-after subject.

In 1941, photographer Yousuf Karsh produced what became the classic image of Churchill: a photographic portrait taken amid war negotiations, allied strategising and political stoushes.

Churchill had just delivered a speech to the Canadian Parliament, following which he was brought to the Speaker's Chamber. Unbeknown to Churchill, Karsh was ready and waiting with his equipment – he had a two-minute window to take his photograph. The resulting image has a powerful directness and intensity of character. Churchill appears angry in the portrait: the consequence, Karsh recounted, of his having removed one of Churchill's precious and perennial cigars from his mouth. Cigars hung from Churchill's mouth as he stood on podiums to address constituents, while he inspected troops in Tripoli, as he walked through the streets of a bombed London. He stares directly at the camera, right hand on a chair, left on his hip. He's not going anywhere.

The photograph was placed on the cover of *Life* magazine in 1942 and quickly became the iconic image. It affirmed Britain's position of strength and lack of patience with Hitler. It also catered exactly to Churchill's image of himself – defiant, well-dressed, in an environment of honour and fully in control as he gazes down upon his audience.

Thirteen years later, the Sutherland portrait, by contrast, denied Churchill the stamp of power and authority that Karsh had gifted him. Interestingly, in another photograph from the session with Karsh, Churchill poses in a decidedly more relaxed disposition. He smiles warmly and contentedly, as though he and the photographer are longstanding friends – his generosity of spirit on show for his public. This changeability of character caused many portrait artists unenviable consternation.

So why was Graham Sutherland chosen to paint this momentous and most public of commissions, Churchill's eightieth-birthday portrait?

The portrait commission was overseen by Jennie Lee, MP, a direct, uncompromising Scottish parliamentarian who had targeted Churchill in her maiden speech in 1929 as 'cant, corruption, and incompetence' and who had experienced a typically tumultuous political career herself.[10] Time had passed, a war had been fought and won, and Lee had mellowed in her views of Churchill. A fee of 1000 guineas was agreed for the portrait to be painted by Sutherland.

Sutherland had spent the majority of World War II on salary with the War Artists' Advisory Committee, his six-monthly contracts continuously renewed. His evocative and haunting paintings of a bombed London have a point of difference from the standard imagery: his desolate, dark, smoky scenes are figureless. War artists' guidelines forbade portrayal of the dead, so Sutherland left the bleak, almost obliterated streets entirely unpopulated – a sign that the life of the city had truly been destroyed. But Sutherland's war service, while commendable, is not sufficient reason for the Parliament's choice. One would expect that for the commission of such a public portrait as that of Churchill, the artist would be eminently experienced in the genre of portraiture.

Sutherland's sporadic portrait output included a picture of the erudite and charismatic Somerset Maugham, whom he portrayed posed on a chair, somewhat elongated in body, using a palette of autumnal tones attuned to Maugham's cultured personality. He also produced a portrait of a seated Lord Beaverbrook, Churchill's Minister of Aircraft Production, and although Beaverbrook claimed he did not like the portrait, he also considered it very good. He is understood to have recommended Sutherland for the Churchill portrait and a number of studies by Sutherland of Churchill can be viewed in the Beaverbrook Art Gallery in Canada.

Perhaps the commissioners wished their choice of artist to reflect the risk-taking that Churchill had exhibited throughout his life: risks within his war strategies, financial risks, political risks, risks in his journalistic writing, challenging political strategy of the day. Yet Sutherland was popular with art critics and fellow artists. Sir Kenneth Clark described him in a catalogue essay published prior to the Churchill commission as:

[an] outstanding painter of his generation . . . no English painter since Constable has been received with so much respect in the critical atmosphere of Paris.[11]

Sutherland had represented Britain at the 1952 Venice Biennale, enjoyed successful shows in Paris and New York, and in 1953 had an exhibition at London's Tate gallery, with catalogue essays by Sir Kenneth Clark and Herbert Read. (Sutherland's portrait, when finished, was sent to the house of Sir Kenneth and Lady Clark, where Clementine Churchill initially saw it.)

Art historian Peter Fuller described Sutherland's work as:

uncompromisingly contemporary, characterised by a search for imaginative transfiguration, a desire to redeem sacred nature, bombed cities and mutilated men and women through the exercise of aesthetic transformation.[12]

Many would have agreed that Churchill needed some 'aesthetic transformation'. He was still Prime Minister of Great Britain, but at eighty years of age, a war veteran and a survivor of fifty-four years in politics, and not in the best of health – the years had worn him.

'Are you going to paint me as a bulldog or cherub?' Churchill asked Sutherland.

'That depends on what you show me!' Sutherland replied.[13] He was not going to allow Churchill to absolve himself of the outcome.

Sutherland relied upon his ability to keenly observe and distil an evident humanity. Churchill, with his noble birth, his heroic military service and his strategic political leadership, seemed invincible. Yet Sutherland, with his meticulous intimacy of interaction with his subjects, saw somebody else within the glamour and power of Churchill's exterior. He stated many years later:

> The question of likeness, of course, goes far beyond the simple question of physical likeness. One draws or paints in a way which one's emotions always direct.[14]

Churchill was not always secure in his decision-making, was not always untroubled and had, like us all, experienced loss and immeasurable grief. The artist was interested in the internal fight of the man rather than the external heroics and public recognition, which were better defined by Churchill himself. (Churchill always ensured he received his battle medals, for example – his letters remonstrating with his mother, on occasion, to chase them up.)

The portrait cannot be considered a sign of disrespect by the artist for his subject. Sutherland and Churchill had much in common. Sutherland, the son of a lawyer, had studied engineering before he decided upon a career as an artist. He began his career quite conservatively in the world of romanticised etchings of landscapes, before moving into paintings that aimed to garner an emotional response to the views he chose to portray.

Landscape painting was Churchill's field, and no doubt the portrait sittings were punctuated with discussions of technical matters and treasured vantage points around the house.[15] Putting aside their obviously common experience of war, the two men's interests also extended to multifarious wanderings and French society. Churchill's beloved south of France had also captivated the Sutherlands for many years as a holiday destination. Indeed, a year after the portrait was completed, they purchased a house in Nice to find some respite from the controversy and notoriety.

Sutherland wanted to ensure that his portrait was a response to the personal rather than the public Churchill. There was to be no association with war gallantry, power and idolatry. He had seen the soul-destroying results of war. There would be no gleaming medals or polished brass, nor the golden epaulettes of a military uniform. Sutherland's war service had taught him the vulnerability that an elegant uniform of office could hide, and he understood that his job as an artist was to find the insecurities, not conceal them. And portraits of Churchill in uniform and formal dress were plentiful.

Sutherland was attempting to uncover the person who roamed somewhere beneath Churchill the performer, the man whose public display was the daily fodder of newspapers [Figure 4]. It is possible that Churchill, who had famously and audaciously once recited the words to Hamlet from the front row of the theatre in unison with Richard Burton on stage, was not aware when performance overtook his constant self. He had summoned a nation with his commanding radio broadcasts and believed his voice carried a message for all to hear – at all times.

Sutherland's job was not an easy one. In addition to all of the complications of painting a character such as Churchill, he had to navigate painting the portrait of a fellow artist, albeit one often publicly self-deprecating as to his technical ability. When Sutherland arrived for the first sitting with just a small notepad, Churchill remarked abruptly, 'Young man, you do not have the right kit!'[16]

Churchill had not started painting until he was forty years of age, making his output of over 500 paintings substantial – given his other slightly pressing tasks during this period! And it was not to politics that he intended to devote his time in the afterlife, but the far more illustrious pursuit of art:

> When I get to heaven I mean to spend a considerable portion
> of my first million years in painting, and so get to the bottom of
> the subject.[17]

He later confirmed this statement and expanded upon his intentions in his 1948 publication, *Painting as a Pastime.* It was the puzzle of the landscape that appealed most to Churchill. The dominant subjects of his paintings are his beloved gardens at his country home, Chartwell Manor, and the magnificent southern French landscape that had attracted the Impressionists. He did, however, produce a number of self-portraits that are illuminating.

Churchill's self-portraits provide further evidence of his commitment to the performative. While self-portraits traditionally offer an insight into psychological states, artistic identity and self-examination, Churchill's few self-portraits gravitate to evocative memories of his artistic life and signs of his society.

As he stated in his 1922 publication in which he philosophises and muses over the subject of painting:

> Painting is a friend who makes no undue demands, excites to no exhausting pursuits, keeps faithful pace even with feeble steps, and holds her canvas as a screen between us and the envious eyes of Time or the surly advance of Decrepitude.[18]

Probably the most informative of Churchill's self-portraits is the early wispy full-length study from 1919–20 in which Churchill presents himself as artist. In his painting smock, holding his palette and looking at us as though he searches to understand this world in which he finds himself, the insignificance of the figure within the picture plane is notable. The abyss of brown paint that surrounds him almost absorbs his small figure, suggesting insecurities that were not simply attributable to the brush. This is a private view that was not for public presentation. It bears a strong similarity to the work of Walter Sickert, the artist and friend whose sketch of Churchill had been so cavalierly destroyed by Clementine. Most specifically, it is reminiscent of Sickert's stage performers, who often appear lost among the lights and costumes that consume them. Sickert achieved a considerable painting career but still found time to assist Churchill with his various painting problems.

Another of Churchill's self-portraits amusingly presents Churchill from behind in the act of painting. His *Sir Winston Churchill Painting Under the Loggia at Chartwell* (1927; private collection) shows him leisurely pursuing his passion, the springtime blossoms in the distance. He continued his focus on the self-portrait in 1927 with the intriguing view of his society. *Tea at Chartwell, 29th August 1927* (1927; National Trust, Chartwell) centres upon a floral embossed tablecloth covering a round table laden with tea paraphernalia, designed to satisfy the nine well-dressed guests who have gathered around it to imbibe, chat and, in a break from engagement with each other, turn to gaze at us. In the midst of the blue monochrome work sits Churchill, turning to greet us as though we, too, have arrived to join the table.

The painting is also a statement about the regal qualities of his society. Viscount Cherwell is present, as are Sir Edward Marsh and the enigmatic Diana Mitford. Present also is Sickert and it is likely that his 1927 portrait that Clementine destroyed was undertaken at this tea party. The portrait was perhaps designed to be a kind of aid to assist Churchill with his own painting – allowing him to study the application of colour, the brushstrokes and the framing of the figure.

Sutherland chose to paint the portrait at Chartwell Manor, Churchill's country home, specifically to remove Churchill from the gentility and ceremonial identity of London and to place him within the spaces of his wife, his leisure, his animals and his paintings. It was here that Churchill quietly fished, walked, exercised his desire to be an artist and dined with family and friends. It was a respite from the cut and thrust of politics.

Churchill and Clementine had developed a fascination for the looming brick residence in 1922. The magnificent view it afforded over the Weald of Kent – the south-east gardens of England – is known to have inspired many a poet, diarist and scientist. Importantly, it could offer a quiet retreat from the pressure and torment of city life for the large family.

Chartwell was set upon 32 hectares of grounds, with a sparingly modernised Victorian red-brick house that required significant renovation, and Churchill spent two years hiring architects, builders and gardeners to achieve his vision for his home. The venture became a labour of love and one he remained attached to, seeking out the beatific pleasures and solitude of the quiet environs throughout the majority of his political life. He designed lakes and rose gardens and even constructed the brick Orchard Cottage next to his studio 'with his own hands', as the accompanying plaque reads. The studio is placed among a group of cottages situated some distance from the main house, separating Churchill from the site of his domestic, political and literary lives; his study accompanied the main bedroom.

Sutherland and Churchill could wander from the main house across the lawn to the studio and equally immerse themselves in the solitude of nature. There is no doubt that the degree of comfort afforded by the isolation, the expanse of nature that was at the height of its summer offerings and the opportunity for Churchill to once again observe the practice of a professional artist would have contributed to the image of Churchill that Sutherland observed. This was not a two-minute pause in between applauded speeches in Parliament. Sutherland's response was far more considered and enveloping, giving due and developed regard to the complexity of Churchill's personality.

During the portrait sittings, an opportune visit by the photographer Elsbeth Juda resulted in an archive of observations of the artist–subject interactions. The National Portrait Gallery holds a number of her contact sheets from the portrait sittings [Figure 5], and these show that Sutherland's wife of twenty-seven years, Kathleen Barry, a former fellow student from Goldsmiths' School of Art, was also present and acted as his assistant. She can be seen sitting in place of Churchill while Sutherland worked to find the right pose, but there are also many images of Churchill seated in the manner that reflects the final portrait. Some capture his particularly glum look, while others offer a relaxed Churchill, cigar in hand, seated with his dog in front of his paintings, either staring down at the camera or in posed shots gazing into the distance.

Juda, with her husband, Hans Juda, published the British exports magazine *The Ambassador*, which gave artistic credentials to images of industrial design. The promotion of British wares no doubt found support in the eyes of Churchill. Juda had actually travelled to Chartwell Manor to photograph Sutherland, but naturally saw in the portrait sittings a subject matter of interest. The photographs were also ultimately used by Sutherland as support material for the painted portrait.

Summer slipped into autumn during Sutherland's visits to Chartwell. With Churchill still Prime Minister, time was not in great supply, and with every beat of the great man's fingers Sutherland worked to complete the preparatory drawings and sketches that would inform the final portrait. A number of these sketches survive and provide evidence of Sutherland's ideas for the portrait and his response to the changeability of Churchill's personality throughout the course of their sessions.

A head study in oil, *Winston Churchill* (1954; National Portrait Gallery, London), conveys a great deal about the shadows cast upon Churchill that Sutherland witnessed. It is clear that Sutherland had no intention of a heroic vision of his subject, searching instead for the deeply personal.

Photographs taken of the final portrait when the body and surrounds were beginning to emerge from the marks of paint – the face still blank – show that the artist had issues with the original placement of the hands. He had assigned Churchill's hands to his knees, with the left hand gripping the striped trousers in a tense spread-eagle of fingers, causing the fabric to fold in unison with the fingers. Interestingly, at the ceremony to present the portrait to Churchill, he sat in exactly that pose upon the podium while waiting for the curtains to reveal the portrait.

It may have been the change to the pose that created an unease for Churchill. For the final painting, Sutherland introduced curved arm rests onto the chair, providing Churchill with a prop to lean on. In the preparatory photographs, it is possible to observe Sutherland adjusting Churchill's hands to fold over the armrest. In the final painting, the fingers curl around the ends of the arms of the chair, leading the eye to the fleshy tools of Churchill's trade. They reflect Churchill's age and his imaging of himself at Chartwell as the workman, the fingers appearing somewhat stubby and awkward – as though they truly belong to a labourer rather than to the erudite Prime Minister.

The 1943 portrait of Churchill by Arthur Pan which hangs in the American Embassy in London provides an opportune comparison with Sutherland's portrait. Pan's picture is of a seated Churchill, complete with cigar, and his hands are elegant and refined, with long fingers that would grace the keys of a piano more appropriately than the trowel of a bricklayer. The attitude is smug and serious, while the background is bare, as is that of Sutherland's portrait.

34

Portrait artists will often provide the paraphernalia of a life as a support to defining the character of a subject: a compass for an explorer or a paintbrush for an artist, for example. But unsurprisingly, Churchill was too great a personality for such superfluous details. And interestingly, the majority of portrait artists throughout his life treated him the same way. An early 1916 portrait, *Winston Churchill* by William Orpen (National Portrait Gallery, London), painted following the disastrous Battle of Gallipoli, is a fine standing portrait of a desultory Churchill against a blackened background – symbolic of the chasms of darkness that haunted him. There is no cigar in the Orpen portrait – too great a sign of opulence for the Irish artist serving a commission in the Army Service Corps.

Sutherland equally made a decision to forsake the cigar. He agreed with his portrait predecessors. Better to deny Churchill his apparatus of presentation, strip him as much as possible of any accoutrements, in order to present the personality of the man.

Sutherland's compositional strategy of removing the hands from gripping the knees opens up the figure and allows the eye of the viewer to traverse Churchill's body in considered contemplation. Churchill can be scrutinised – from the hem of his tailored Henry Poole & Co. pinstripe trousers, vertically through the line of his waistcoat buttons to the obviously de-centred spotted bow tie, and up to the withered flesh of his throat and the dimple in his chin, finally ending at the kink in his nose.

It is this placement of his self as an object of scrutiny that most upset Churchill. Bereft of the pose that defined his image – a pose so confident that it obscured any signs of vulnerability – Churchill appears in this portrait somewhat lost. One discovers Churchill's face, a face that is more like the contours of a map than one of the most identifiable faces in the world. Finally, it is to the eyes of the man that our focus is led. They have, at the age of eighty, receded into their sockets and fight the wrinkled skin that competes with the habitual authoritarian pierce of his gaze.

Sutherland has not bothered to please Churchill. His lack of regard for the stature of the man speaks to us, the viewer, of the intimacy of interaction between artist and subject rather than the notion of historical posterity that Churchill desired.

The day of its unveiling was not, of course, the first time that Churchill had seen Sutherland's finished portrait. His wife, Clementine, had viewed the picture first at Sir Kenneth Clark's home and had sent a photograph to Churchill, no doubt concerned as to his reaction. Then the portrait had been delivered to No. 10 Downing Street a week before the public unveiling. If he chose, he had plenty of time to contemplate the work.

He would have expected a portrait of a face that flickered with his life – a summation of his achievements. A face that reflected the tumult, the devastation, the glorious victories, the might of the British Empire that the twentieth century had experienced. He would have wanted us to recognise ourselves in his portrait – to hear his speeches to the masses to keep fighting, to remain strong and to unite against Hitler, to remember where we were when armistice was declared, to mourn those we had lost. He was his own muse, absorbed by his achievements.

Instead, he was faced with the image of himself as 'a down-and-out drunk who has been picked out of the gutter in the Strand', he concluded to his private secretary Anthony Montague Browne.[19] Sutherland had the gamut of art history to draw upon, yet, according to Churchill, he failed in bringing that to bear upon his portrait.

So, rather than humbly stand in Westminster Hall on that day in 1954 to accept the portrait, along with other birthday gifts and accolades from his fellow parliamentarians, Churchill chose, in his amusing and erudite way, to remind everyone in his speech of his service to the nation.

The day began with English roses, birthday cakes and presents from world dignitaries arriving at No. 10 Downing Street. Reporters flooded the pavement to record a smiling Churchill as he emerged to make his way to the opening of Parliament, full-bodied in his winter overcoat beneath threatening skies. He appeared in the best of health and spirits – the BBC film footage recorded his salute to the reporters with the removal of his top hat.

Onlookers waited by the side of the road in their raincoats; the Queen arrived wearing 'a glittering coronet of pearls and diamonds', according to the BBC commentary, to open the fortieth British Parliament, during which she traditionally asks for God's blessing upon her Ministers. Yet the Queen was not present when the commanding portrait was unveiled to the Members of the Houses of Commons and Lords and invited guests in Westminster Hall. It is the manner in which Churchill commenced his speech following the portrait's unveiling that provides particular insight into his self-reflection and the extraordinary coming together of all parties to honour him. He proclaimed:

> This is to me the most memorable public occasion of my life. No-one has ever received a similar mark of honour before. There has not been anything like it in British history.

Considering the many achievements of his life, he clearly believed that it was in the summation of his life that posterity would rest. He continued:

> I doubt whether any of the modern democracies has shown such a degree of kindness and generosity to a party politician who has not yet retired . . .

Upon this statement, laughter flooded the Hall – and Churchill stopped to receive the response in the style of a well-honed comedian.

In the multitude of photographs of Churchill, he rarely appears other than extremely disgruntled. He began perfecting this pose at the age of seven, updating it throughout his life with a parade of social gestures indicative of his power and success. Yet, like his clever management of the portrait unveiling, it was all a performance: what Shakespeare referred to as the 'insubstantial pageant'.

The solemn temples, the great globe itself,

Yea, all which it inherit, shall dissolve,

And, like this insubstantial pageant faded,

Leave not a rack behind. We are such stuff

As dreams are made on, and our little life

Is rounded with a sleep.

The Tempest

We are created from nothing, shine as brightly as is possible and, in the process of returning to dust, wonder at the dreams that thrill and torment us. Churchill excelled in the pageant of life – in the display of brilliance of his strategic mind and, of course, his irrepressible style.

He would not allow himself to be remembered by a 'remarkable example of modern art'.

CHAPTER 2

An Artist's Choice: Adolf Hitler

Imagine you decide to paint a portrait of Adolf Hitler, years after his death, having lived through World War II yourself.

It would truly be a daunting task. His face is a menace that threatens to consume any painting. And the work would have to do justice, somehow, to your experience of the scale of the war's damage and desecration.

But why would you choose to do it? Would it be an attempt to expunge your trauma by transferring it to canvas – a psychoanalytical foray into your pain? Or would it be a reminder to all of the horror of Hitler's dictatorship? His face, like it or not, is inescapably tattooed upon the psyche of the world's population; no matter how many years pass, its lines still mark horror and destruction.

Perhaps your portrait would present him macabrely immersed within the millions of deaths he caused: an image of his day of reckoning. The souls of all those who perished in gas chambers, or were raped and murdered in their homes, or shot at the foot of mass graves – they might surround him like a *Game of Thrones*–style army of the dead. Or your portrait might be the antithesis of the heroic images of Hitler, posed in the traditional manner with his hand on his hip, gazing into the distance with the full authority of his position – unless you wanted to remind everyone of the process of seduction.

Perhaps you might choose to paint Hitler the moment before his suicide on 30 April 1945, with the knowledge of his defeat written clearly upon his face. In those final days of April there was no doubt as to how the war would end for Germany. The Russian Army's artillery was deliberately and ferociously pummelling the New Reich Chancellery, the seat of Hitler's rule: its magnificent marble gallery and Hitler's 400-square-metre office were reduced to sites of mass confusion as his imploding army sought shelter among the fine furnishings and imposing marble-topped tables, the huge glass windows exploding with shell fire.

The advancing Soviet army's treatment of Hitler admirers was known to be horrific, so pictures of Hitler were placed into the street to be spat on, kicked and broken; women, fearing rape and murder, tore up portraits of Hitler along with any photos they had of their uniformed husbands.

It had been during the final stages of the long, bleak war of evil that Hitler and his advisers, on 16 January 1945, chose to descend the steps, hidden almost ten metres beneath the Chancellery complex and formal gardens, into the pit that was the *Führerbunker*. There was little change to Hitler's routine of daily meetings and personal obligations in comparison to his life above ground, a routine that included gazing upon the face of his hero Frederick the Great, the portrait by Anton Graff one of the few decorative items he took with him. It was in the *Führerbunker* that he and his advisers cowered, attempting to salvage a victory while others fought and died for Hitler among the chaos and new ruins above.

Constructed as a symbol of the Third Reich's glory and power, the New Reich Chancellery was intended to mark the commencement of a great age of Nazi rule – it was prophesied that in a thousand years, the building's ruins would provide the same pleasure as the completion of the edifice had in 1939, in time for Hitler's fiftieth birthday. Hitler's influence was the magnificence of the Roman Empire, the ruins of the Colosseum; his obsession with the notion of the ruin could be the starting point for your portrait. You'd want him to be in the midst of contemplating the ruin of his nation and experiencing the fear of the end of his life – a fear he had inflicted on so many.

In 1962, seventeen years after the war, Dresden-born contemporary artist Gerhard Richter took up his oils and painted a portrait of Hitler based on a black and white newspaper photograph [Figures 6 and 7]. Richter could have chosen any one of thousands of photographs that proliferated during and after the war, but he selected an image that showed Hitler at his finest hour: addressing one of the Nuremberg rallies, most likely the one in 1934.

The picture shows an animated yet controlled Hitler, mid-speech, at one of the rallies designed to inspire and unite the German people. Hitler was appointed Chancellor in 1933, and yet by 1934 he had ordered a program of extravagance in both staged events and the built form, as signs of the dawning of his great age. The rallies ran their course over eight days, each day dedicated to a display of power from military ranks, Hitler Youth marches, troopers and so on. Hitler often gave up to twenty speeches, speaking of Germany becoming great again, of the need for sacrifice, imploring hundreds of thousands of people to work to support their German origins.

Architect Albert Speer (known as 'the Nazi who said sorry') had been appointed 'Commissioner for the Artistic and Technical Presentation of Party Rallies and Demonstrations', and arranged astonishing light shows to accompany Hitler's performances. His most spectacular endeavour was surrounding the mass of people at the Zeppelinfeld at Nuremberg with 130 anti-aircraft searchlights beaming into the night sky. They were columns of light into the future: an image of the empire that Hitler envisaged. (Speer would later design and construct the New Reich Chancellery.)

Richter did not choose a picture of the leader posed with the Nazi salute, or passively standing to purvey his armies and lands, as was common in the propaganda. Instead, he depicts Hitler in a moment of strangulated shouting, hysterically commanding, his face elongated and distorted. The decision was a remark on Hitler's astounding ability to sway his armies and citizens to fall in behind him, committing the most horrific atrocities. His power lay in his command of a crowd.

There is a hint of craziness, of trauma in Hitler's face: this is no calm, solid statesman. Yet his authority is evident in the adroit placement of his right arm across his body, a gesture Hitler had practised as a sign of resistance and power. It was akin to the American hand-on-heart gesture; indeed, Richter may have been mocking such actions in his choice of this photograph, as the hand-on-heart was adopted by Americans in 1942 as a replacement for the traditional Bellamy salute to the American flag. The Bellamy salute, it was agreed, was too similar to the Nazi *heil*, the German salute.

Nuremberg had been an obvious location for the rallies. It's considered to have been the capital of the Holy Roman Empire in the twelfth and thirteenth centuries, with Hitler's hero Frederick the Great assisting in the development of its trade routes. Hitler referred to the period of the Holy Roman Empire – from 800 to 1806 CE – as the First Reich. Of course, he would also have been mindful of the pogroms in the thirteenth to fourteenth centuries that resulted in the massacres of many Jewish people.

The Zeppelinfeld at Nuremberg was also the site for Leni Riefenstahl's 1935 film *Triumph of the Will* that showed the rest of the world the might of the German army, and Nuremberg was famously the site for the International Military Tribunal trials in 1945–46, where many of the perpetrators of the evil were sentenced to death.

Richter exhibited his *Hitler* portrait for the first and only time in 1964, in an exhibition in the garden of gallery dealer Rolf Jährling with fellow Capitalist Realism artists Sigmar Polke and Konrad Lueg. The show was intended to persuade Jährling to exhibit their work in his Galerie Parnass, and in this they were successful – but Richter did not include the *Hitler* in the later show. Perhaps he was confronted by the idea of exhibiting such a controversial image in the formal setting of an indoor exhibition. What began as a protest exhibition, and perhaps a protest painting, became more than Richter could publicly announce.

Sometime afterward, Richter destroyed the portrait, most likely by cutting it into pieces although he has been deliberately guarded as to the means of destruction. The act may be comprehensible in one sense – artists edit all the time – yet why would a young artist invest so much time, skill and sincerity into a work only to destroy it?

The power of the political portrait is generated through meticulous repetition. To this end, Hitler employed a coterie of 'court painters' – although surprisingly, considering that his image was vital to his campaign, he was not interested in posing for the artists. They had to rely upon approved photographs.

Fritz Erler was one of this group, a painter whose posters had gained popularity in World War I – the most famous being an image of a trench soldier covered in mud, heroically gazing towards the future. Erler produced portraits of Hitler regularly between 1937 and 1944, and his enormous *Portrait of the Leader* was presented at the *Great German Art Exhibition* of 1939. (These exhibitions were essentially propaganda exercises, showcasing images of warfare and socialist idealism as well as of the men who led Germany's military and industrial spheres.) The portrait shows Hitler in his brown tunic uniform and swastika armband, standing in front of a classically styled sculpture of a seated black male figure, his hand supporting an eagle preparing for flight. Erler copied the image from a 1931 photograph by the official Nazi photographer, Heinrich Hoffmann – a man who had ingratiated himself to the Nazi regime with such efficiency that he was Hitler's favourite.

Hoffmann's archive of images of Nazi hierarchy is an extraordinary resource; many of his photographs were used on propaganda posters and postcards, as well as being source material for sanctioned artists. Some of the most notable Hoffmann photographs, however, were not meant to become public – they are candid images that show Hitler trying out various poses to use during his orations. In the 2003 film *Hitler: The Rise of Evil*, Robert Carlyle in the role of Hitler mimics the gestural actions that created the image of leadership to the world. At one point, with eyes closed, he recreates the famous Hoffmann photographs of Hitler in which he prepares himself to inspire his followers. For the viewer all these years later, the photographs of Hitler are strangely compelling; Hitler appears as though midway through the performance of a contemporary dance piece. There is no doubt that he would not have wanted to provide such an insight into his construction of power.

The known official painted portrait of Hitler from life, Heinrich Knirr's official 1937 portrait, is a classic example of Hitler's standard image. He is heroic, in a stance of authority with one hand on his hip, in army uniform and gazing directly and seriously at the viewer. It's a look of unflinching power, designed to transfix and secure devotion: the hand on hip a sign of work, and the direct gaze designed to both appeal to a public and undermine an enemy. It's not unlike Churchill's poses in his official portraiture – the styling of Stalin's images is likewise similar. It is as though they are all playing to type.

In addition to the standard militarised portrait, there were other photos that supported the image of Hitler as the complete man – for example, at dinner parties or with groups of children. Naturally, any official portraits needed to be approved by him, and there were photographs he tried to suppress – of his face distorted into an awkward smile, of strange poses in lederhosen and long socks in the German landscape. One 1930s propaganda publication, *Deutschland Erwache*, shows Hitler in his shorts, smiling and gazing at children – images he later banned.

Like Churchill, Hitler was also an artist. It is an aspect of their lives that provides for an interesting comparison. Both were audacious leaders, fearlessly taking action and often denying the advice of ministers or generals. To be an artist also requires a certain audacity, as placing one's 'talent' on a public stage can be daunting, perplexing – accomplished artists often nervously work in such a space. It also requires the ability to think deeply about oneself, or issues or the social environment. Reconciling these attributes with the war directives of both Churchill and Hitler is not easy. Yet both desired, ultimately, to be artists; that was their strategy for retirement.

Hitler also played at the role of the cultural aesthete, concomitant with his campaign to depict himself as the supreme human being who could lead the world – better than everyone in every way. It was a philosophy in line with the Nietzschean notion of the Superman (*Übermensch*). Hitler had paid homage to the philosopher through visits to the Nietzsche-Archiv, where he was, of course, greeted by Nietzsche's sister upon arrival. She had control over Nietzsche's writings after his death, and Hitler was the manifestation of everything she would have the world believe of his philosophy; comfortable with this view, Hitler construed Nietzsche's statements as suppliant to his image. The following words by Nietzsche are typical of those that found favour with Hitler's belief in his supremacy:

> It is my fate that I have to be the first decent human being: that I know myself to stand in opposition to the mendaciousness of millennia.[1]

Reconfigured to indicate the supremacy of the Aryan race, it was able support for a hierarchy of human existence that had Jewish people and ethnic black people at the bottom. The writings of Nietzsche promoted the concept that man (and it could only be man, not woman) should strive to be greater than he is, including culturally. Supremacy constituted the parting of the oceans of otherness to make way for the Aryan race, and everything should be done to ensure it reached its potential.

As writer Frederic Spotts has it, Hitler used culture to buttress his power; while power, of course, gave him the opportunity to enact his dreams.[2] He was the great German Romantic incarnated as an Aryan beast, and drew on the music of eighteenth-century composer Richard Wagner to socialise the notion of death as a reward. Wagner's message of honour obtained via the spilling of blood could be found within the strains of *Siegfried's Funeral March*: those who died for their country were to be idolised and rewarded with posthumous honour. Wagner's music was played at the Nuremberg rallies; Hitler drew sustenance from it.

The image of the cultured man was also conveniently used by Hitler and his inner sanctum as propaganda to smother any association with their atrocities. The objective was to exult in the glory of the nation, rather than dwell on the means of achieving it.

The old adage of sprinkling a little stardust to hide the detritus was not lost on him. There were gala dinners and balls with sweeping chiffon gowns; pretty young Eva Braun, in her shimmering satin dress, beside her hero in his standard brown tunic; the sparkle of the military uniforms of the generals; Wagnerian concerts; art exhibitions and grand receptions. There were photographs with the famously banished Duke and Duchess of Windsor who we now know had ingratiated themselves to Hitler, and with artists, actors and singers who swooned within Hitler's inner circle, helping to convey the magic of the new age. The populace, exhausted by the effects of war, lapped up the parade of glamour as a momentary escape.

Respect for Germany's cultural prowess was an important component of the Third Reich leadership. Indeed, Hitler cared so much that in March of 1945 he ordered his *Hitler-Jugend* (Hitler Youth) to hand out potassium cyanide capsules following a performance of the Berlin Symphony Orchestra; musicians should also be allowed an easy death should it come to that – the supported death by suicide that many in Hitler's inner circle chose for themselves and their precious families.[3]

For the young Gerhard Richter, images of Hitler and the Nazi regime would have been difficult to avoid. There were propaganda posters plastered everywhere, including the famous poster *The Hand that Guides the Reich*, showing the Nazi salute to the youth of Germany. The poster, which had been copied from the extraordinary 1934 painting *The Flag Bearer – Hitler in Armor* by Hubert Lanzinger, also permeated German households. In it, Hitler is depicted as the supreme saviour – dressed in silver armour in the style of a knight from German tales, sitting astride a horse, and holding a flag bearing the swastika. It is a fabricated identity, as Hitler did not parade on horseback – it was not an image he promoted – yet the painting was exhibited with approval at the *Great German Art Exhibition* in 1937. Perhaps Hitler enjoyed the new persona; his face by this time was well known to his community, so his identity could be played with and recast to complement the ideology.

During the long, bleak war, the display of the Führer's image had protected people, as is common with portraits of dictators – indeed, it gave non-supporters a cover. Homage to the portrait and a greeting with the *heil* were signs of allegiance, and a citizen's failure on either account was potentially dangerous. The Gestapo was incapable of watching everyone, particularly as support for the war waned, and relied upon the public to report seditious behaviour. As the Nazi regime crumbled, of course, deserters were tracked and killed, usually by hanging in public view. And at the end of the war, Hitler's propaganda was vehemently destroyed, although some was treated as memorabilia by soldiers of the Allied forces, or simply left to decay among the ruins. Photographs by German artist Herbert List of museum sculptures surrounded by bombed-out buildings record the faded glory of the Third Reich – a ruin that had arrived far too early in Hitler's plans.

The Lanzinger painting, like many of the artworks produced under Third Reich guidelines, now sits deep in the archives of the US Army Center of Military History. Confiscated at the end of the war, it escaped the destruction that was the fate of many artworks, but was pierced with an American soldier's bayonet: the hole in the oil panel just below Hitler's eye has never been restored. It's an apt symbol of a Führer who was steadfast in his pursuit of glory yet oblivious to the turmoil that surrounded him.

Public images in support of Hitler have remained taboo in Germany since the three major powers of Great Britain, the United States and the Soviet Union established, in the final throes of the war, the Potsdam Agreement of 2 August 1945. The issue of borders was their primary concern, but the agreement also ensured that Germany would be 'de-Nazified'. The confiscation of the Lanzinger painting and 8722 other military-associated items was in accord with the agreement, which bestowed the right to 'destroy the National Socialist Party and its affiliated and supervised organizations, and to dissolve all Nazi and militaristic activity and propaganda'.[4]

Germany resolved to resist all attempts to rehabilitate the former leader: until recently, displaying a portrait of Hitler was only (realistically) achievable outside of the country. There have been a few guarded exceptions, one being the 2010 exhibition *Hitler and the Germans* at the German Historical Museum in Berlin. In order to prevent any considerations of idolatry on the part of viewers, however, the curators chose to present the portraits in miniature; the enormous propaganda posters glorifying Hitler and his compatriots were, quite deliberately, missing. In a similar manner, Richter's choice to destroy his portrait of Hitler may have been influenced by his concern that he could be misaligned with the former leader's views.

In 1950, some 1659 non-military and non-political pictures were returned to Germany, but it required a request from the German government for a further 5850 to be returned in 1986. Even so, the US military retains a collection that it deems could revitalise the Nazi spirit. The majority of these works are portraits or swastika-imbued propaganda; there are also four watercolours by Hitler himself.

Hitler remains the most researched and scrutinised of leaders, his life and leadership of the Nazi regime constantly paraded within our visual and literary landscape. It's rare that a week passes without further exploration of his ignominious desire for power; his war strategies; his mental health; his sexuality; his advisers; the sustained loyalty of his compatriots. And the merest hint of oligarchical desires in contemporary leaders draws immediate comparisons with him.

Retribution remains swift for any public impersonation of him, or use of the symbols associated with Nazism. In Germany, the *heil* is a criminal offence, even if the perpetrators have no political intention in executing the gesture – in 2017, Chinese tourists were arrested by German police for mimicking the act. Even outside of Germany, reference to the salute is considered inappropriate: in August 2017 CNN commentator Jeffrey Lord was fired for tweeting '*Sieg Heil!*' More than sixty years after the end of World War II, the memories remain unresolved and, for many, imbued with the emptiness of those lost in battle or through incarceration.

At Madame Tussauds in Berlin, the wax image of a slumped and angry Hitler is permitted due to its containment, both artistically and literally: it has been placed within a small room designed to appear like the *Führerbunker* so that visitors cannot 'stand beside the Führer' and no photography is allowed. The current approach to the exhibition of the figure, visible only through a window, is in response to the vandalism that occurred when the exhibit first appeared. At the opening of the Berlin Tussauds in 2008, a visitor known as 'Frank L.' raced past the security guards as the doors opened, shouted 'No more war!' and ripped the statue's head off in outrage. He was applauded in Germany for 'decapitating Hitler': the fact that this was a statue, not the ruler himself, was almost irrelevant in the rhetoric that followed. Sixty-three years after Hitler's death, to 'Frank', destruction of the work was his only means of taking revenge.

For Richter, too, there is substance to the view that in his destruction of his *Hitler*, he was taking the only revenge he could on behalf of those who died around him, for the lives that had been destroyed. Did he destroy the portrait so that he could take back a semblance of lost autonomy?

Richter, like most German people of his time, experienced the war through both his own involvement and that of his family. Born in 1932, he was only seven when British Prime Minister Neville Chamberlain sat in front of a radio microphone and delivered his *Ultimatum Speech*, declaring that his country, having received no undertaking that German troops would withdraw from Poland, was at war with Germany.

Richter joined the obligatory Hitler Youth organisation and 'played' at war like all kids, pretending to fight armies in the forests around his home, excited by the notion of combat. Indeed, it was the forest that held an attraction to the Third Reich as symbolic of the fundamental nationalist qualities to which they desired a return within German society. Hitler believed that the core of German nationalism and historical memory could be found within the German forest. Historian Simon Schama has investigated that under the Third Reich, German children were trained in forest ecology, the notion of survival and the preservation of indigenous species finding favour with right-wing ideology.[5]

In 1943, Richter's resourceful mother, Hildegard, decided to move her young family out of their home in the German town of Reichenau, near Dresden, to rural Waltersdorf, some distance from the main action. Richter played within earshot of the firing guns and listened to the details of Russian, British and American advancements upon Germany.

The move was a wise one, as in February 1945 the city of Dresden was controversially bombed, the initial order given by 'Bomber' Harris of the British Bomber Command. Estimates are that 25,000 people lost their lives over the hours of the Allied bombing raids – the people of Dresden were not the perpetrators of Hitler's evil, but their destroyed city and charred, faceless bodies were a result of it. The destruction of Richter's birthplace was a pivotal moment. Years later Richter commented that he had been able to hear the bombings although also doubted that it was actually possible from Waltersdorf, attributing his memory to the radio broadcast.[6] But family members were caught within the city, unable to escape, and the horror of the destruction was combined with personal loss and repulsion.

Of course, Hitler would have wreaked similar destruction had he been able. From his bunker, he had instructed Speer to adopt a scorched-earth policy should the war be lost – he didn't want anyone else to reap his country's riches. Luckily, Speer didn't always follow orders and was able to thwart the dissemination of Hitler's wishes to the German hierarchy.

Meanwhile, Richter's schoolteacher father, Horst, had been one of the hundreds of thousands of German men drafted into the military in 1939. He was initially sent to the Eastern Front, to engage in one of the largest and most devastating battles in history: it's believed that 30 million people died there, whether in battle, massacred, during internment or simply due to living within the battle zones. Richter's father survived; his reward, in 1943, was to be sent to the 700 kilometres of trenches that made up the Western Front. Captured by the Allies, he spent the remainder of the war in an American prisoner-of-war camp.

When Horst returned from the war, he was both defeated as a soldier and unable to resume his profession as a teacher – anyone associated with the then-despised National Socialist Party found it impossible to participate fully within society, and was certainly not permitted to teach children. His only options for employment were menial and servile; he eventually obtained a position as a labourer in a textile mill.

Richter observed his father to be a broken man and adopted his mother's opinion of him. She had, as historian Dietmar Elger noted:

> . . . nothing but reproach for Horst, given his failure to distinguish himself, going so far as to intimate to young Gerd [Gerhard] that Horst may not even have been his father.[7]

A later portrait of Horst by Richter, *Horst mit Hund* (1965), is permeated with this sense of failed masculinity. The blurred image of Horst trying to hold an out-of-control dog is an image of disappointment; Richter is bereft of pride, and so he portrays his father as somewhat silly.

Richter's uncles Rudi and Alfred were not as fortunate as his father, having been killed in the war. His Aunt Marianne also did not survive. Living with a mental illness, she had been placed in an institution at the age of eighteen, making her perfect fodder for Nazi eugenics policies. She was part of the initiative that undertook large-scale euthanasia under Hitler's T4 program, which disposed of (among others) people with disabilities or mental illnesses, essentially those who were considered detrimental to the establishment of his master race.[8] They were transported to one of the isolated killing centres, assessed by doctors and put to death usually through gassing and cremation. Smoke from the chimneys was a permanent fixture on surrounding horizons.

As Hitler's power was derived from his command of mass audiences, the scale of the stadiums in which he orated his speeches was a masterful counterpoint to his humble plea to be considered as the common man. This was an image reflected in his brown uniform, adorned with his Iron Cross and Wound Badge from World War I and his gold Party Badge. It contrasted with the threatening black *Schutzstaffel* (SS) uniforms. It was the ability of Hitler to manipulate power and secure his appeal to the people that provided him with the apparatus to govern over the most horrific atrocities. The Final Solution was never discussed publicly during the war, although Hitler had been purging Jewish people from government, business and the arts since he was appointed Chancellor. Other eugenics programs, similarly, were covered up and glossed over as 'treatment', the victims' cause of death falsified.

Richter, like many German citizens who had lived through the war, had much to reconcile in both his life and work. It begs the question: If you, like Richter, had been compelled to follow Hitler, and your father had been required to fight on his behalf, destroying the very fabric of your family, how would you feel personally towards him? How would you convey that feeling in paint? And why, having navigated the parameters of your portrait, having solved the puzzle of how to convey all those years of torment and horror, would you then destroy the picture?

For Richter, the connection to the *Hitler* was fraught. It had the potential to influence his hope for the future – it was a work that could define his memories of a blackened and traumatic past. Hitler had been omnipresent throughout half of Richter's life – perhaps the portrait was a means to expunge him from memory, to paint and destroy? The act of destruction allows the release of a stultifying hatred, achieves the personal, physical sensation of purging that hatred. Yet it may also have been due to concern about the work's impact – in 1962, Nazi ideology continued to circulate within some quarters, while the pain and horror associated with the war was still a raw and recent memory.

At the end of the war, Richter was given a small plate camera by his mother and, inspired, started down the path of a career as an artist.

Like all artists, he experimented with the self-portrait. The blunt and unresolved impact of the war upon Richter, and his struggle to find direction, is manifest in a watercolour self-portrait from 1949, when he was seventeen. Haunting, dark and lit from beyond, it is imbued with a fear that stems from Richter's sense of himself as isolated and distinct from those around him. While all of Germany struggled to reconcile the atrocities of the war, Richter, whose life was steeped in familial experience of war, Nietszchean ideology and artistic ability all within the setting of East Germany, established a divergent means of survival. In his self-portrait, one eye is fully exposed to the viewer, while the other remains in darkness, indecipherable. As one of the few surviving portraits from this period, it provides an insight into the desolation of war and its impact upon one artist.

The self-portrait facilitates the gaze upon oneself through the image presented in the mirror, the overlay of the trauma of war intensifying the impact of what is reflected. Artists find liberation in the production of the self-portrait, and the intimacy of the undertaking allows for an experimental style of portraiture that can often produce a sense of theatricality. Richter's contemplation of himself provides the viewer with the opportunity to consider the manner in which he viewed his appearance. His self-portrait appears staged, as though the lighting is artificial and designed to create dichotomies of sight and protracted visibility.

In 1951, Richter's career path led him back to the rubble of Dresden with his acceptance into the Dresden Art Academy. His birthplace had been all but obliterated, a mere shell of its former self – irreconcilable with his childhood memories of the cultured, middle-class setting of his mother's literary and musical pursuits. To return there, to rediscover Dresden as a city of people forcing their way through and around the ruins, like seeds flowering after a fire, affected Richter. He remarks:

My time in Dresden fundamentally and powerfully influenced me, although I wasn't really aware of it at the time. I realized it later.[9]

The art practice that he was able to explore in Dresden was far from ideal, of course. The new German Democratic Republic (the 'GDR', or East Germany) was then governed by the Socialist Unity Party, and the party dictated artistic product – choosing to glorify Communist leaders like Lenin, Marx and Engels. During his five years at the Academy, Richter learnt to paint in the narrative Social Realist style, and was required to demonstrate his allegiance to state-sanctioned subject matter by producing numerous propagandist posters of Stalin.

Richter was most successful in applying this style of art to mural painting, and was employed to execute a number of state works containing the political message of a healthy, structured society. His *Joy of Life* mural at the Deutsches Hygiene-Museum and *Workers Uprising* at the headquarters of the Socialist Unity Party are reminiscent of the work of his artistic heroes, Mexican muralist Diego Rivera and Pablo Picasso. (Both were followers of Stalin, and therefore their work was permissible, in spite of its frequent lack of realism.) It is in particular the figurative narrative style of Rivera that is clearly an influence upon Richter's life-size depiction of families engaging in healthy activities in the first mural, and his representation of the working-class's battles against the oppressors in the second. The essentially propagandist murals provided Richter with the opportunity to understand the impact of projecting a political message on such a scale.

Neither of Richter's murals are now visible. The *Workers Uprising* was lost, and the *Joy of Life* was painted over by authorities in 1979 – prompted, it is understood, by Richter's criticism of the participation of Social Realist artists in *Documenta 6*, an exhibition of contemporary art that occurs every five years in Kassel, Germany. Richter withdrew his paintings over a disagreement with the curatorial direction of the 1977 exhibition.[10]

Renovation of the Deutsches Hygiene-Museum in the 1990s could have included removal of the paint covering the mural, but did not. Richter himself considers exposing the mural to be a waste of money: he is happy that it remains out of view, 'destroyed'. It is a work that connects to his historical past, a formulaic rendering of life in Germany. In 1958, Richter commented that he never took the bureaucratic process seriously, desiring a greater artistic freedom.[11] Richter's analysis of its significance as well as his later response to the *Hitler* portrait provide an opportunity to consider his connections to the present/past historical, the ambiguity of both works residing in his satisfaction with their destruction.

Interestingly, art historian John Curley has identified one of the couples portrayed in *Joy of Life* as Richter and his first wife.[12] Perhaps this is part of the reason behind his contentment regarding the mural's destruction.

In 1959, when he was twenty-seven, Richter attended *Documenta 2*. The town of Kassel is situated close to the former GDR border and thus it provided those confined in the GDR the opportunity to experience the contemporary art of the West. Richter, for the first time, was able to gaze directly upon a substantial collection of the work of major artists of the twentieth century, many not previously exhibited in Germany. Richter, as a state-sanctioned mural painter, had been one of the privileged citizens who could freely undertake trips to West Germany and internationally. The travel he undertook was to further his practice and investigate new techniques, with the existentialist heart of Paris one of his destinations prior to 1959. His freedom meant he became acquainted with the experimental, creative practice of the West but, until *Documenta 2*, he had found little to impress him.

The Nazi regime had imposed strict controls upon the display of modern art: the *Entartete Kunst* or *Degenerate Art Exhibition* of 1937 was famously designed to expose modern art's inanity. It was referred to as the 'art of decay' and 650 examples of confiscated artworks were offered to the public to support the premise. Following the exhibition, over four thousand works considered 'degenerate art' were burned in Berlin, while much later in Paris a bonfire outside the Jeu de Paume museum in the summer of 1943 destroyed hundreds of works by Paul Klee, Picasso and Max Ernst among many others – there were ninety works by Picasso on the inventory, although some were kept and sold by the Gestapo and some much later restored to their rightful owners.[13] The burning of these works and Hitler's hatred and public association of 'degenerate art' with Jewish people was analogous to his treatment of people in the Final Solution.

The control over the display of modern art was sustained into the period of the Soviet-controlled GDR, and a range of art styles was generally banned, including art considered to fall within the framework of the subversiveness of German Expressionism; work influenced by avant-garde Western trends; and, of most concern to the controlling power, art conducive to fantasising about a freedom of spirit.

It is difficult to imagine the response of the visitors from East Germany when confronted with the extraordinary colours and paint application of the Abstract Expressionists. The small black and white reproductions they were used to, collected from magazines and postcards, were revealed as gravely inadequate once they stood before the works in all their majesty.

Documenta 2 included works from artists who had fled the terrors of Germany or been deported due to their subversive practice, as well as from the heroes of American art – artists as diverse as René Magritte, Wassily Kandinsky, Jackson Pollock, Robert Rauschenberg, Helen Frankenthaler and Francis Bacon were on display. (The controversial 1955 work *Bed* by Robert Rauschenberg was to remain in its crate, however.) The colour and size of the works and the dramatic engagement with the rules of abstraction astounded Richter. He was able to consider the work of Kandinsky beside Pollock, to trace the lines of influence, of points of departure in the sweep of American art. He was particularly excited by Pollock's ability to prosecute the act of painting, the manner in which he covered the total canvas and explored a world beneath the surface of a postwar society. Richter was ready to find a new dimension to his work, and his frustration with the constraints upon his painting now became painfully obvious.

It is now known that the work of the American Abstract Expressionists was promoted internationally as part of a Cold War offensive by the CIA: supporting the GDR's avant-garde left was one of the most effective ways of counteracting Moscow's oppressive approach. The freedom, scale and individuality of the work contrasted with the heavy traditional subject matter and rigidity of GDR artwork – confirming the rhetoric that America was moving forward in a spirit of democracy and engagement, that it was the most sophisticated creatively that it could be. The CIA had (covertly) established the Congress for Cultural Freedom following the war and identified artists and writers to promote; Pollock was a particular favourite because his work robustly signalled America as innovative and cultured.

Richter later stated that it was the viewing of the Pollock paintings at *Documenta 2* that influenced him to leave the GDR.[14] The CIA had worked their magic on an artist who has since become one of the highest-selling contemporary artists. An enlightened Richter realised that he needed to escape the constraints of GDR governance, and his opportunity to prepare for his defection came in March 1961, during a train journey to Moscow and Leningrad (St Petersburg). The train fortuitously stopped at West Berlin station, providing Richter with the time to place a suitcase in a station locker before continuing on his journey. He returned to East Germany only long enough to collect his wife, Ema, and a small number of other possessions, and, travelling on the S-Bahn train, managed to enter West Berlin undetected. The Richters stayed in a refugee camp for eight days before reuniting with Ema's parents, who lived in Oldenburg.

Sadly, Richter would never see his own parents again; he wrote to his former professor:

> . . . it was very difficult for me to go, even though I knew I had to act; I am aware of what I have left behind.[15]

A few months after his defection to West Germany, on 13 August 1961, the Berlin Wall literally went up overnight; Berlin would not be reunited for another twenty-eight years.

With his enrolment in the West German Düsseldorf Academy in 1961, Richter began to experiment with the Western styles he had managed to witness to varying degrees throughout the 1950s. He recalls, 'I painted through the whole history of art towards abstraction', immersing himself in testing the application of paint in the manner that had so excited and invigorated Western art.[16] Yet satisfaction with his efforts in the 'Art Informel' style (the French approach to gestural, Abstract Expressionist painting) did not come easily, and he chose to burn his experimental works from 1961 and 1962 in the middle of a courtyard in 1962.

It is notable that Richter chose the most absolute method to destroy these early pictures, just as Lady Churchill's secretary had done with the Churchill portrait. It was also an action reminiscent of the public burning of books by the Nazi regime.[17]

In 1962, with the objective of finding some common ground between his training in East and West Germany, Richter began to seriously experiment with photo paintings – the practice of taking photographs from popular culture or his personal archive and copying the image in paint. He was exasperated with the abstract notion of painting and considered the copying of photographs to be a relief. 'Moronic' was the word he used to describe his photo paintings; yet he considers his career to have commenced in 1962 with this approach, perhaps because this was the most innovative he had been to date.

Using readily available black and white photographs, Richter embarked upon a series of works in the early sixties of transposing images as he saw them. Richter's photo paintings include family, Pope John XXIII (which he later burnt), frolicking partygoers, aircraft bombers and President Lyndon B. Johnson consoling Mrs Kennedy following President John F. Kennedy's assassination.

It is no surprise that Richter's new artistic direction should lead to a series that also included *Hitler*. The damage of Hitler's war had ultimately manifested in a brick-and-wire wall that cut right through the heart of Germany. No matter that Hitler had died seventeen years previously; Richter, like many, needed to explore the desecration of life and freedom through his creative practice. Everything in his life had been directed to that moment. The work relates to his experiences of war, to his trauma and to his family.

The choice of image is pivotal in Richter's work. It is often the strangeness and the banality of his selection of images that provides an insight into the issues, style, culture and obsessions of society that captured his attention. In a 1964 letter to gallerist Heiner Friedrich, however, Richter wrote:

> I also can't explain why I actually paint a photo, in general and in particular a certain photo; what it is that I find enormously fascinating; and what meaning the representational has for me.[18]

It is hard to accept, however, that the choice of Hitler was arbitrary or that the meaning of the act for Richter was not consistent with his war experience and that of his family.

Richter collected the photographs in his *Atlas*, a supremely sophisticated scrapbook in which landscape scenes are juxtaposed with photographs of discarded charred bodies of victims of war, Holocaust scenes, and family portraits collected and smuggled across the border. It is, essentially, an artwork, the 'backend' of his catalogue of exhibited works.

Richter commenced *Atlas* in 1970, yet the first pages are devoted to images collected in 1962, the year he designated as the start of his painting life. In these pages sits the photograph on which he based his painting of his father, Horst. The source photograph for the *Hitler* portrait could also have been included in the ten pages of *Atlas* dedicated to 1962, the year it was painted, but it was not. This was not unusual and there are a number of paintings for which the source material is missing.

Richter only returns to the subject of Hitler seven years later, in the 1969 pages. He includes a montage of pictures relating to Hitler: scenes of masses of people surrounding a flag emblazoned with the swastika (the German flag from 1935 to 1945); Hitler posed in the delivery of a speech, at dinner and in propaganda photos with groups of children. These are all juxtaposed against a photograph of the empty Mosaic Hall in the New Reich Chancellery, indicative of the emptiness of battle and Hitler's crazed vision for a restored golden age. There is also a picture of 'The Eternal Guard' at the Temples of Honour in Munich. This was Hitler's sacred place, the place of rest for Germany's heroes – eternal solace for those who had freely given their lives for the common good. (Like many of the shrines to Hitler's philosophy, this structure was destroyed following the war due to its potential to become a beacon for Nazi followers. Hitler's bunker was also destroyed for this reason, concreted out of existence with the most unheroic grey carpark.) Richter also includes a page of photographs from 1970 of Nazi locations in Nuremberg – overgrown and left to crumble, exactly as they should be.

Despite the omission of the source material from *Atlas*, Richter places the *Hitler* at number three in his *catalogue raisonné* (or catalogue of works); by contrast, he eschewed his other destroyed artworks and the murals he produced in the GDR. His control over the account of his artistic development, defining his work in 'self-authorized catalogues' and extensively documenting his oeuvre on his website, is not unusual for an artist, according to Stefan Gronert.[19] Strangely, when he provided an overview of his past work in 1968, Richter referred to the *Hitler* as one of a rather passive group produced in 1962 and 1963: 'some of them still picturesque and sentimental: Stag, Castle, Hitler, etc.'[20] It is difficult to reconcile the *Hitler* with this description, although perhaps his reference to the sentimental may be to his childhood during the war and his desire to see his family. He also suggests here that the painting may still have been in existence in 1968.

Richter's portrait of Hitler is inextricably bound to his experiences during the war and the trauma inflicted upon him and his family. Richter has often commented that while it may appear every subject is open to him, there are things that are unpaintable because they are easily understood. But in the process of painting Hitler, and of looking at the painting during the years he possessed it, the complexity defeated him. He knew that this was not someone 'easily understood'. His rendering of the portrait in a Pop art style suggests that this was a means of tackling the subject, yet Richter could not reconcile the superficiality of the image with the depth of his life experience.

In a portrait, the choice of sitter, pose and styling are indicative of the artist's character – in this way, a portrait can convey an uncanny resemblance to the artist, posing the idea that each portrait is also a self-portrait. No doubt, in the case of a Hitler portrait, this is a horrific thought.

Richter's 1949 self-portrait was one of the very few known portraits he completed before he began the black and white pictures of the early sixties, but from that point, portraits were omnipresent in his work. His portraits, according to art historian Robert Storr, expose a great deal about the German experience:

There is nothing in German painting of the time that presents the continued Nazi penetration of daily life so matter-of-factly, so unflinchingly, or from so many sides of the German experience.[21]

Richter's life experiences provide an opportunity to reflect upon the impact of Hitler's war-mongering on German citizens. His family portraits are a precious resource of unusual insight, made obvious through comparisons to the formal clarity and pop-culture approach he took with *Hitler*.

Richter painted the portraits of his Uncle Rudi and Aunt Marianne in 1965. The portrait of Marianne shows her as a young girl, smiling to the side of the picture frame. In front of her lies the four-month-old Richter, straddled across a pillow. Marianne's sweet short-cropped hair and the glistening pearly white innocence of the scene, compositionally reminiscent of a *Pietà*, belies the tragedy of her life. Richter frowns in the way babies often do at the world, confused by the commotion, wishing only to be cocooned within the mother. But Richter does not settle on Marianne's fate with this portrait – he continues the narrative with the portrait *Herr Heyde*, also painted in 1965. Richter's blurred image was taken from a newspaper photograph showing the capture of Dr Werner Heyde, the Nazi who was one of the main organisers of the T4 program responsible for his aunt's murder. Following the war, Heyde lived under an alias until his arrest in 1959; five days before his trial in 1964, he committed suicide. The circle, for Richter and his aunt, was somewhat complete.

The portrait of Rudi is a familiar image of an uncle smiling as anyone would in a family snapshot – yet he is cushioned within his

Nazi overcoat and slanting helmet in front of the abrupt, angular lines of a bleak, functional building. The upper storeys rise above an aged fence, contrasting with the scraggly branches of a tree that has managed to just survive in the inhospitable environment.

The sociality of the portrait, the 'pressure to conform to social norms' as art historian Richard Brilliant identifies, is present here in Rudi's pose and Richter's choice of image.[22] The heavy black boots weigh Rudi down; the soft smudging suggests both Richter's relationship to the clearly loved uncle and the fleeting nature of his life. Rudi would last only a few days in the battlefields before being killed: Richter has marked Rudi's territory within his homeland for the last time, with Rudi oblivious to his fate. He doesn't present as someone full of vigour and strength, either: his masculinity is not constructed in this photo according to the propagandist ideal of the German army. It's strangely antithetical to the numerous images of Hitler, in which he rarely smiles or appears to encourage engagement. Rudi belies the image of the Nazi regime – an image that Richter was perhaps keen to dispel on his family's behalf.

In order to provide a measure of atonement for the actions of his uncle in his role of Nazi soldier, the portrait was presented to an exhibition commemorating the atrocities committed by German troops in the town of Lidice, Czechoslovakia. Richter, on behalf of his uncle, was apologising.

There is nothing of the blurring of *Onkel Rudi* or the glistening spectacle of *Aunt Marianne* in Richter's portrait of Hitler; it is painted with harsh, exacting outlines. Richter has followed the path of Hitler-approved artists by painting his portrait from a photograph

– indeed, one that Hitler would most likely have approved. There is no sentimentality in the picture, no yearning for a past, no questioning of his existence. Hitler was there and destroyed Richter's homeland. Richter makes no attempt to humanise him, and the black and white colouring suggests both the journalistic reporting of a past event and the loss of aesthetic realism. It imbues the image with banality.

So, could Richter's portrait of Hitler be considered within the same context as his family pictures? Is it an alternative signifier of the complexity of life for German people, a desire for recognition of the individual choices made by people who were consumed by the dictatorship of one? Rudi gazes at us, confronting, probing and questioning, his nervous demeanour engaging us emotionally in his imminent departure for war.

The Hitler portrait is a statement of Richter's life as opposed to an illustration of it. It references the propaganda portraits of Hitler he grew up with, the family members killed in war and the need for all those displaced by war to retrieve a trace of normality of life. He did not meet Hitler, he did not fraternise with the Nazi regime, and so this work is a political statement, with the face of the leader personifying the impact of the entire regime. Rather than using a slogan, Richter has employed the body to announce that impact upon his own life. One body, one simple man, upon another and another and another.

Richter painted the image of Hitler again, this time twice on the one canvas. The portrait comprises a mirror-image of itself, as though Hitler was speaking above a pool of water. Hitler reflecting upon Hitler – who before us is the most evil man in the world?

Richter painted over this canvas with cream paint and on the reverse side, in 1963, painted *Stag (Hirsch)*. While seemingly disparate subjects, Hitler was often photographed patting deer near his home in the Bavarian Alps, part of his propaganda that associated him with the beauty of the natural German world, the wider populace initially believing in this message of a passive, uncomplicated man.

Richter's response to his portrait of Hitler exposes both the significance of portraits of leaders and the complexity of response to an image of a face. Contemporary artist Hans Weishäupl's 2008 *Faces of Evil* series provides a helpful perspective here. To create the works, Weishäupl took photographs of 350 people from each of a dictator's countries and then pieced together components – someone's nose, another's wrinkled brow – to create photographs of faces that resemble each of the dictators. There is an uncanniness about the portraits: Weishäupl is asking if there isn't just a little of the dictator in all of us.

He places the focus upon the face – on the idea that it is possible to find evidence of the dictator in the features. But would we so readily follow someone who looked very different to the majority? Do we need to recognise something of ourselves in a leader?

Weishäupl's *Hitler* is perhaps the most disturbing picture. It is an aged face, suggesting his appearance some twenty years after he died. The greyed hair is still parted on the side, but the eyes sense the horror he created. Or is that Weishäupl's desire – that Hitler could not have lived another twenty years without some acknowledgement of his atrocities?

CHAPTER 3

Presidents
and
Dictators

One can never predict the response to portraits that accurately observe, rather than flatter, their subject. Powerful people, in particular, are less than pleased if a portrait fails to communicate their authority.

In 1877, Thomas Eakins painted the portrait of President Rutherford B. Hayes seated at his desk, working – a fitting pose for a president, one would think. The Union League of Philadelphia, who had assisted in Hayes' campaign for the White House, had commissioned the portrait; the league had portraits of Washington and Lincoln among other admired leaders, and they wanted to add one of their favourite sons. Unfortunately, the portrait lacked the necessary heroic appearance. It showed Hayes as somewhat flushed due to the heat of the August day in Washington when Eakins undertook the portrait. The club members and critics were bemused and offered that it looked as though he had been drinking, a strange assertion given that he was famous for banning alcohol from the White House and, indeed, his wife was commonly known as 'Lemonade Lucy'. After its initial exhibition in the Union League's rooms, the portrait was given to the President (unbeknown to Eakins) – and was never seen again.[1]

Hayes was not the only one of Eakins' sitters to be dissatisfied. He was often accused of enhancing age, features or behaviour to the point that he had mothers weeping, sitters embarrassed and daughters worried about the family legacy. A number of his (often exaggerated or desultory) portraits were hidden or destroyed by the subject or their family, not wishing descendants 'to think of their grandfather as resembling such a portrait'.[2] Others also reacted violently towards some of his portraits. A portrait by Eakins of one of his students, Edward W. Boulton, was slashed by a waiter and had to be repaired by Eakins – it was ultimately destroyed in a fire. Commissioning a portrait from Eakins became a fraught enterprise, particularly when he sometimes refused to part with the finished product.

By comparison, over a quarter century later in 1903, French society painter Théobald Chartran seemed like a fine choice to produce a portrait of incumbent President Theodore 'Teddy' Roosevelt Jr [Figure 8]. He had previously painted a well-received though slightly awkward-looking seated portrait of Roosevelt's predecessor, William McKinley, in 1897 (now in the Carnegie Museum of

Art) as well as the *Painting of US and Spain Signing Peace Protocol* (1899) held in the White House collection. Chartran also painted portraits of Roosevelt's wife, Edith, and daughter Alice in 1902 to much acclaim and the Roosevelts' delight. Commissioned by the French government, these two latter portraits were presented to the Roosevelts as gifts and were widely exhibited, including at the 1902 Paris Salon. The portrait of the First Lady, sitting in the White House gardens wearing her usual couture designer dress and a wide-brimmed hat, was most popular.

Chartran, having had experience of the Roosevelts, was not intimidated by the formality of White House life, which could have otherwise deleteriously impacted the portrait. Chartran was also fortunate in that he encountered a good-natured President; Roosevelt had an energy and complexity of character that would surely place him as the most desirable of subjects for a portrait artist. He was a formidable man, often described as robust and headstrong, with a background that included a degree from Harvard University and study at Columbia Law School as well as public and military service. He came to the attention of the Republicans after leading the First US Volunteer Cavalry, known as the 'Rough Riders', in the Spanish–American War of 1898, and was quickly promoted through the political ranks. When President McKinley was assassinated in 1901, Roosevelt, as Vice President, succeeded him and became the 26th President of the United States.

Roosevelt had a great deal to contend with in taking up the presidency, with an agenda that included ending the isolationism of American trade and retarding the formation of the large conglomerates that reduced competition. His vision of a prosperous trading future also led him to advocate for the secession of Panama from Colombia, paving the way for the US to take over construction of the partially completed Panama Canal.

Photographs of Roosevelt show him as vigorous, smiling beneath a bountiful moustache that became his signature accoutrement, and often peering inquisitively at his public through thinly rimmed glasses. His great energy can be seen in the photographs of his 1904 election campaign speeches: almost jumping out of his skin, facial muscles taut as he makes his argument. He was a favourite of caricature artists, courtesy of his former life as an all-hunting western-style cowboy, and well into his presidency was still depicted in illustrations wearing a cowboy hat, polka-dot bandanna and gun holster. He'd positioned this way of life within an intellectual and patriotic construct of the American man by writing books on hunting and pioneering experiences.

During the 1904 election campaign for his second term, according to biographer Aida Donald, Roosevelt was:

> touted as a writer and a scholar, not a warrior, and he was called the man who most represented the spirit and values of the twentieth century.[3]

He had clearly come of age and grown into the presidential suit comfortably during his first term in office.

While Roosevelt pursued an image of American masculinity closely linked to outdoor pursuits, he was not immune to expressing his emotions – as long as they were couched appropriately. His bountiful correspondence records his sensitivity and care for his family. One letter dated 1 February 1903, written to his thirteen-year-old son, Kermit (who was at school in Massachusetts), shows Roosevelt to be a surprisingly hands-on father, describing his pillow fights with his two younger sons and reading to them in the evening if Edith was too tired. Roosevelt paints a picture of lively domesticity among his large, noisy family, expanding on the accomplishments of 'Mother' (Edith) as a hostess and even describing the colours of her many dresses.

The letter also included a brief, blunt mention of Chartran's work: 'Chartran has been painting my portrait. I do not particularly like it.'[4]

Chartran had posed Roosevelt in the White House garden – perhaps attempting to allude to his pioneering spirit – but he looked quite out of place. In the portrait, Roosevelt leans upon a stone fence in the garden, holding his pocket watch in his right hand, with his left fist on his hip. But Chartran loses us with Roosevelt's gaze, which extends over the viewer's left shoulder as though into the distance. In the portrait, the President appears the dilettante, with time literally on his hands – not the man who could work twelve hour days and hike through Yellowstone National Park. This was not the image of a president who could defend America, fight the trade wars and win the next presidential election.

The painting of an official portrait of a US President is news, no matter the century. The *New York Tribune* of 4 January 1903 reported

Chartran's arrival in America to paint the President's portrait (among other commissions). The *Washington Post* of 22 January 1903 recorded that Chartran had paid a visit to the White House, while the *Washington Times* of 15 February 1903 anticipated that the Roosevelt portrait would be displayed at the annual Knoedler Gallery exhibition of Chartran's work, alongside his 1902 portrait of Roosevelt's daughter Alice.

High expectations for the portrait, unfortunately, were not met, and when it was exhibited at the April 1903 Salon of French Artists, critics slammed it. Journalist Gaston Stiegler wrote that he 'saw only a very ordinary business man in an ordinary suit . . . with nothing in the face to show a genius to grasp problems concerning nations'. Another critic wrote scathingly that the portrait looked like a hurried photograph, and that 'no one would dream of discussing the artistic merit of this smooth and clearly painted portrait'.[5] Yet another concluded that the portrait was a failure because 'the head of a great nation, is not sufficiently prominent'.[6]

Chartran must have been devastated by the negative response. He had retouched the painting in Paris prior to its exhibition at the Salon but was unable to 'rescue' it and chose to attribute the poor result to Roosevelt's lack of availability for the portrait sittings, political and family interruptions making it very difficult for both parties to concentrate. Some years later, Roosevelt had, it seems, learnt the lesson of devoting enough time to ensure a portrait was a success. In 1908 the wealthy industrialist and art collector Charles Lang Freer (of the Freer collection) commissioned Gari Melchers to paint Roosevelt's portrait. Roosevelt indulged the artist, with three-hour

Figure 1 Diego Velázquez (1599–1660), *Las Meninas*, or *The Family of Felipe IV*, c.1656, oil on canvas, 318 × 276 cm. Inv.: P01174. © 2019. Image copyright Museo Nacional del Prado © Photo MNP / Scala, Florence

Figure 2 Graham Sutherland (1903–1980), *Winston Churchill*, 1954, oil on canvas, 147 × 121 cm (destroyed). Photo by Larry Burrows © Larry Burrows Collection

Figure 3 Sir Winston Churchill speaking in Westminster Hall, on his 80th birthday, 30 November 1954, photograph, 36.1 × 29.3 cm. Image: PA Images/Alamy Stock Photo

Figure 4 Graham Sutherland explaining the work on one of his studies of Sir Winston Churchill at the exhibition, 'Portraits by Graham Sutherland', 6 June 1977, photograph, 37.5 × 47 cm. Image: Keystone Pictures USA/ Alamy Stock Photo

Figure 5 Elsbeth R. Juda (1911–2014), *Winston Churchill*, 1954, bromide contact sheet, 25.3 × 20.4 cm. Image: National Portrait Gallery, London

Figure 6 Gerhard Richter
(born 1932), *Hitler*, 1962, oil on
canvas, 110 × 130 cm (believed
to have been destroyed).
Image: Gerhard Richter Studio

Figure 7 Hitler addressing
Nuremberg rally, c.1934,
photograph. Image: Imperial
War Museum

The photo was printed
on the front page of the
Daily Mail, 1 May 1945, to
announce the death of Hitler.

Figure 8 Théobald Chartran (1849–1907),
Portrait of President Roosevelt, 1903,
oil on canvas (destroyed). Image: Miriam
and Ira D. Wallach Division of Art, Prints
and Photographs: Print Collection, New York
Public Library

Figure 9 John Singer Sargent (1856–1925),
Theodore Roosevelt, 1903, oil on canvas,
147.6 × 101.6 cm. Image: White House Collection/
White House Historical Association

Figure 10 Stalin statue demolished by the Hungarian patriots, Budapest, 1956, photograph, 22.4 × 33.9 cm. Image: Cola Images/Alamy Stock Photo

Figure 11 A wanted poster of Robert Mugabe outside Zimbabwe House, London, as Zimbabweans demonstrate calling for free and fair elections, 27 June 2008, photograph, 16.9 × 25.5 cm. Image: Thabo Jaiyesimi/Alamy Stock Photo

Figure 12 *Bearded Man, Possibly Emperor Macrinus,* early to mid-3rd century CE, carved Luna marble, 26 × 17 × 22 cm. Harvard Art Museums/Arthur M. Sackler Museum, Alpheus Hyatt Purchasing Fund, 1949.47.138. Imaging Department © President and Fellows of Harvard College

Figure 13 *Bronze Portrait Bust of a Roman Matron (Agrippina),* c.20–50 CE, bronze. Edith Perry Chapman Fund, 1952. Image: The Metropolitan Museum of Art, New York

The bust is considered to have been a dedication, possibly part of a shrine in a family home.

Figure 14 *Lower Part of a Statue,* c.1479–1458 BCE, diorite. Rogers Fund, 1931. Image: The Metropolitan Museum of Art, New York

The work dates to the joint reign of Hatshepsut and Thutmose III. While there is no inscription, the smashing and dumping of the figure suggests it is a statue of Queen Hatshepsut.

sittings interspersed with shorter periods and Mrs Roosevelt often on hand to keep the President company should he become bored – and to avert another disaster.

Interestingly, however, Chartran did not destroy the work himself – as he did when criticised over another portrait. The painting was one of his typical commissions, a portrait of a wealthy American man's wife: when the husband proclaimed that he thought the work splendid but could see no likeness to his wife, 'Chartran laid down his brush and, taking out his penknife, slit the canvas into ribbons, after which he bowed his critic out'.[7]

Upon the Roosevelt portrait's return from Paris, the President quietly hid it from view, apparently hanging it in a dark upper corridor of the White House. It continued to appear in the media for some time, of course. On 19 January 1904, the *New York Tribune* mentioned it in an announcement of Chartran's arrival for his Knoedler Gallery exhibition, though the writer did not comment on the picture's whereabouts. Six months later, on 5 July 1904, the *Daily Mail*'s review of his exhibition in London similarly noted that Chartran had painted Roosevelt's portrait but made no further comment, choosing to ignore the blight of the Roosevelt portrait in its praise of 'M. Chartan's [sic] claim to rank with the greatest of modern portrait painters'.

In researching a portrait that is believed to have been destroyed, there is always a measure of doubt – an inkling that perhaps those ordered to act secretly kept the work hidden for their personal benefit. When one imagines the vast corridors, basements and attics of the White House, the doubt increases. In the case of the Chartran portrait, however, the evidence for its destruction was attested to by one of the most trusted aides in the White House: Major Archibald Butt.

A former journalist who had enlisted first in the US Volunteers and then the Regular Army, Butt was called upon to accept the post as Roosevelt's military aide in 1908, and was one of Roosevelt's most trusted companions in the final year of his presidency.

When Roosevelt departed in 1909, the newly elected William Howard Taft asked Butt to stay on; when Roosevelt decided to run for re-election in 1912, the personal conflict led Butt to take six weeks' leave to evaluate his position. Unfortunately, he booked his return journey on the R.M.S. *Titanic*. As testament to Butt's commitment to duty, President Taft stated in his eulogy that he knew Butt would have remained on the ship's deck 'until every duty had been performed and every sacrifice made that properly fell on one charged . . . with responsibility for the rescue of others'.[8] It is, therefore, reasonably difficult to question the reliability of Butt's account of the Chartran portrait's destruction.

In 1909, the Roosevelts were preparing for their departure from the White House after eight years of collecting all the typical array of family paraphernalia, as well as an enormous bounty of presents and souvenirs. Attics were cleaned out, chipped china disposed of and spaces peacefully ordered for the new incumbent.

The Chartran portrait hanging in the upper corridor caused much angst. Butt wrote to his sister-in-law Clara on 7 February 1909 that

'Chartran was no more fitted to paint Mr Roosevelt than I would be'. But it was one of Roosevelt's children, remarking that he looked like a 'mewing cat' in the portrait, that set the President into a spiral of discontent. Butt reports that the family discussed what should be done with the portrait, and when no one wanted it, Edith Roosevelt spoke the words, prophetic of those later uttered by Lady Clementine Churchill, 'and so I will consent to having it burned'.[9]

A week later, on 15 February, Butt reported to Clara that Mrs Roosevelt had instructed him to destroy the Chartran portrait, along with two others that she personally disliked. The pictures were taken from their frames and 'unwilling to trust anyone else with them, I took them to the cellar myself and placed them in the furnace', Butt records. However, Butt was not completely without temptation; he writes that:

[the] hands in the Chartran portrait were simply marvellous, and for a moment I was tempted to save one of these from the flames, but did not think it was the honourable thing to do.[10]

Almost contemporaneously with Théobald Chartran's picture, the US federal government commissioned another portrait of Roosevelt, by famed painter John Singer Sargent, as part of the official historical series of United States presidential portraits. Roosevelt admired Sargent, and the general feeling was that this would be a fine portrait.

Sargent was well known to American society, he was good friends with Henry James, he stayed with wealthy art collector Isabella Stewart Gardner when in Boston and he had completed portraits of a number of American society women, industrialists, intellectuals, musicians and artists.

Sargent returned to America to paint the portrait at around the same time as Chartran, in January 1903. His visit was ardently announced in the newspapers, with editors excited that 'one of the world's most famous portrait painters' had returned to his native land. The announcement was accompanied by a full-length photograph of the reclusive Sargent, his hands pocketed in his overcoat.[11]

Sargent arrived at the White House, paints and easel in hand, in February 1903. He had chosen a canvas measuring 1.47 × 1.01 metres on which to transfer his sketches, with great anticipation of painting the President directly from life, and enthusiastically commenced work. However, he faced the same problem as Chartran – how to garner the amount of time required for a portrait from a man incessantly busy with work and family? He had only a month. Sargent had been criticised for hurried work before: one critic, for example, remarked on his 1890 portrait of Grace Woodhouse (the future wife of the President's cousin Robert Roosevelt Jr):

> The lady seems worthy of more considerate treatment. So charming a subject might at least have been spared the mortification of the flesh – note the leaden-hued, unfinished right arm.[12]

Sargent was a portrait collaborator – a skill honed after too many false starts and portraits not as engaging as he would have liked. The process, in this case, did not begin promisingly, however. After scrutinising the interiors of the White House, Sargent discussed the setting of the portrait with Roosevelt, but it seems they could not agree on an appropriate background, nor the right angle or positioning of the body.

Sargent had decided not to consider an outdoor setting, in order to avoid a repeat of the Chartran disaster. Roosevelt and Sargent walked through the various spaces of the White House, apparently becoming increasingly frustrated with each other's indecision, until they reached the top of a staircase. Isaac Hoover, one of the house ushers, described Roosevelt turning to berate Sargent – placing one hand on a wooden newel post while the other sat firmly on his hip. It was at that moment that Sargent found his picture [Figure 9].[13]

Sargent immersed himself in his subject's routine in order to understand him better, and to find spare moments to encourage him to pose – even spying on Roosevelt as he moved through the house. As he commented to Isabella Stewart Gardner, it was not an easy commission, and he felt exceedingly constricted.[14] Yet he had managed to find a pose that allowed the President to move within the picture frame, an approach he had adopted in his 1902 portrait of the wealthy Philadelphian Peter A.B. Widener.

Roosevelt was a far more engaging character than Widener, and Sargent worked until he had captured the character of the President. This was not a portrait his subject would bury in storage! Sargent managed to achieve a response to, as Henry James so eloquently put it, 'a certain faculty of brooding reflection'.[15] James was enamoured of Sargent's ability to see 'deep into his subject' and evolve with it.

Sargent's Roosevelt is in very sharp contrast to Chartran's portrait. The former confronts us with his gaze, daring us to look elsewhere; Chartran's President looks past us, failing to engage.

Roosevelt displayed the Sargent alongside the Chartran portrait of his wife, clearly indicating his admiration of the portrait and the obvious approval of his family. Visitors to the White House in 1904 were observed by the *Washington Times* as having a 'deepened interest' in the works, according to a lengthy article on the treasures of the White House.[16] There was no discussion of Chartran's portrait in the article.

Over the course of the twentieth century, the portrait photograph has become the ascendant medium. It is through the work of photographers that we know the personality of a leader – photos of the quiet contemplative moments; of a body striding; of hands outstretched in a moment of affection. And many leaders, particularly in the United States, are meticulous in ensuring a prolific photographic record of office.

The official painted portrait, by contrast, is usually produced after the presidential office is vacated, when the President has time to sit and contemplate their achievements and reflect upon their articulation of power. It is the photographic images that reconstruct our attachment to that leader.

So, when 40,000 negatives from Jacques Lowe's personal archive of photographs of President John F. Kennedy were destroyed in the attacks of September 11, 2001, it is no surprise that conservators spent months attempting to restore the images from 1500 contact sheets that had been separately preserved. The archive of negatives had been stored in a fireproof safe in Tower 5 of the Twin Towers, and while the safe was actually recovered from the rubble, there was nothing inside to retrieve.

Kennedy was a star in the American landscape, eminently and congenially photogenic; he could charm in tandem with his intellect. Lowe was Kennedy's personal photographer (he was not employed by the White House) while Kennedy was still a Senator, and his images provide the narrative of Kennedy's political and private journey. The access Kennedy afforded the photographer was concomitant with his desire for a public face to his private life. As Kennedy once stated, 'We must never forget that art is not a form of propaganda; it is a form of truth'.[17]

The conservators at Washington's Newseum painstakingly reconstructed the magical images for an exhibition of Lowe's work. They spent hours and sometimes days on each image to remove the usual scratch and pen marks that cover a contact sheet – the marks of the decision-making process undertaken to find the quintessential image for publication. They aimed to reverse the destruction of one of America's most important archives of portraits. Their commitment provides the opportunity to reflect upon the gravitas of an image and on the connection we feel to the faces that ignite history.

89

Unlike freely elected leaders, a dictator who takes power – often by force – is reliant upon mechanisms such as military action and strategies of fear in order to retain that power. He inspires an allegiance within his citizens to one person, one face, one view.[18] Thus, no portraits are circulated that do not conform to the structured image: the message is one of stability through the solid image of authority, with a subtext of intimidation.

It was the image of Lenin that most upset John D. Rockefeller Jr when he saw Diego Rivera's mural on the walls of his Rockefeller Center. The mural, *Man at the Crossroads Looking with Hope and High Vision to the Choosing of a New and Better Future*, was commissioned from Rivera in 1932, and he made it clear that his intention would be to construct a mural for the people. Rivera stated:

> the only correct painting to be made in the building must be an exact and concrete expression of the situation of society under capitalism at the present time, and an indication of the road that man must follow in order to liquidate hunger, oppression, disorder, and war.[19]

Rivera disputed that he changed his design to include portraits of Lenin on one side and a frolicking Rockefeller on the other – that, he claimed, had always been his preferred design to be painted on the wet plaster.

The mural was a collaboration among Rivera and his assistants and art students just as it was a reflection, he believed, of the uniting of society. He referred to what occurred as the 'Battle of Rockefeller', with police summoned to guard the work and keep media and the public away; eventually Rivera was ordered to stop, and the mural was covered in large canvas sheaths. Rivera mused that without the controversy, the majority of New Yorkers – not to mention the rest of the US – would not have heard of the mural. He exalted in the battle over a portrait of Lenin, a fight grounded in workers' rights. Requests to remove the portraits were refused, and the mural was eventually chiselled off. The destruction didn't stop Rivera. He used the money he'd received from Rockefeller and painted a series of twenty-one panels in the New Workers' School of New York. He also recreated the original mural at the Palacio de Bellas Artes, Mexico City.

Early photos of Soviet leader Joseph Stalin, with his unkempt hair and strong, directed gaze, contrast with the images of dictators we expect. Pictures of dictators as youths come as a surprise, almost with a jolt of recognition – they look like people we've known or even want to know.

It is when the image evolves into the repetition of standard, approved portraits that we stop looking beneath the mask of the dictator. Ritualised painted portraits to promote Stalin's leadership of the USSR were popular. When he came to power in the mid-1920s, he had established a fierce reputation within the governing Politburo. However, Stalin needed an image to put him on the same level as Lenin, his predecessor. Portrait competitions were held in the early 1930s as a means to secure artists who could paint Stalin in a style conducive to the factory-like production required of them.

Sanctioned portraits would eventually find their way to publishing houses to be retouched and reproduced in books, or as posters or postcards. Following approval by the 'Glavlit', the Main Directorate on Literature and the Presses, a portrait of Stalin could move through to the production phase. However, as historian Jan Plamper has ascertained, the decision to use a particular portrait for propaganda could also be reversed and the published work withdrawn and destroyed or placed into 'special storage'.[20]

The early portraits of Stalin were designed to propose him as the warrior, and there was a committed campaign to ensure all in the USSR understood his service to country. The constructed image then became one of the learned man. A typical image of Stalin shows him with book in hand in front of a library. He gazes to the side, contemplative, to inform the viewer that he uses the knowledge of the past to educate the present. It's a stance that can be traced to the Renaissance and the portrayal of the famous man as wise and learned. Other portraits of Stalin were constructed to show him mid-speech, arguing a point, or positioned in his military uniform gazing into the distance. With World War II and the invasion of Russia by Germany, the domestic portraits were abandoned for images of military might and Stalin's strength.

Stalin was either the intellectual, alone and heroic, or the military man and leader pitched with images of other leaders such as Lenin. Art historian Richard Brilliant has referred to such standardised imagery as 'established repertoires of artistic representation'.[21] As a result, we can often recognise a portrait of a leader or dictator without looking closely – the pose and styling give it away. Meanwhile, USSR portraiture from the Stalin period ensured that red dominated in the many posters.[22]

When Stalin died in 1953, the gradual eradication of the leader from Soviet history and life began. The signs and images that populated streets, political party offices and some people's homes were torn down, covered or destroyed. The process of forgetting commenced with the initial removal. Pictures of a smiling Stalin were taken into the streets and burnt, as were images of Lenin with whom he had often been portrayed in posters. Statues of the former leader were smashed and toppled; perhaps most famously, the images of the Stalin Monument in Budapest in 1956 [Figure 10], during Hungary's October Revolution, are recalled as the moment of change for many.

Yet the cult of personality that Stalin had promoted left many people uncomfortable with destroying the portraits they had lived with for most of their lives. This behaviour of preserving the portrait even extended to some who had suffered under Stalinist rule, whose parents had been tortured and killed; still, they looked to the portrait of Stalin on the mantelpiece as the one constant in a difficult and desolate existence.

What is most interesting, however, is that following the fall of the Soviet Communist regime in 1989, the Hungarian government decided to preserve many of the statues removed from the streets during this period of change and placed them in a museum dedicated to Communist statues and plaques, Memento Park in Budapest. The aim of the park is to encourage critique of the past authoritarian rule, to provide evidence of the visual propaganda of that rule and advertise 'great photo opportunities of Lenin'.

In recent times, too, despite evidence that Stalin's rule resulted in the deaths of millions of dissident Russians and the incarceration and torture of many more, there has been a quiet re-emergence of his portrait within the Russian and Ukrainian landscape. The portrait has been used to adorn buses in Moscow for the Victory Day holiday, and images of Stalin are carried to commemorate his birthday. The portraits displayed usually show him dressed in uniform gazing into the distance, his fireside pipe in hand and a warm, comforting smile on his face.

Interestingly, Emperor Nicholas II, who abdicated and was later assassinated along with his family in July 1917 during the Bolshevik uprising, has received a similar rehabilitation. The evocative 1895 portrait of Nicholas by Ilya Repin, which had been proudly displayed in Mariinsky Palace during Nicholas' reign, was cut from its frame and presumed destroyed during the Bolshevik Revolution in late 1917 – but in 1995 the painting resurfaced, and it now hangs in Russia's great museum, the Hermitage, as part of the art historical lineage of Russian painting.

Portraits of past royalty have often resurfaced according to changes in leadership, and equally the portraits of dictators sometimes manage to survive not only physical obliteration but also memories of past atrocities.

When Egyptian President Hosni Mubarak was forced to resign on 11 February 2011 after three decades of rule, public images of him and his wife were the subject of court action.

A climate of fear had gradually evolved in Egypt over the period of Mubarak's rule, and any disrespect of him, whether in words or by way of damage to his portrait, could be personally catastrophic. Dissidents faced detainment, torture, death. Yet protests had been building ever since Mubarak had banned public gatherings in the 1990s. In 2003, the war in Iraq had resulted in vocal, angry crowds demonstrating their opposition with the removal and burning of a billboard portrait of Mubarak, among other acts.

The world's attention was swiftly captured in February 2011 when thousands of people descended on Tahrir Square, Cairo, to proclaim their right to free speech and a new leader. One of the prevailing images of that protest was the removal from billboards of enormous posters of Mubarak's smoothed face surrounded by his black glistening hair, a portrait that saturated the public spaces. The destruction of the portraits was a clear sign to Mubarak and his military that the people no longer feared him – or wished to listen. Some 846 protestors died in Tahrir Square fighting for freedom during that period.

Yet, after the change of leadership, images of Mubarak largely sustained their position in the streets and public buildings of Egypt. So, a lawsuit was filed – and two months after the protests, in April 2011, Judge Muhammad Hassan Omar ordered the removal of Mubarak's name and portrait from public spaces. He declared that their prevalence within the public space resulted in 'tremendous harm and continuous suffering' for the families of the protesters who had been killed.

When Zimbabwean President Robert Mugabe finally resigned in November 2017 after thirty years in power, the anger directed at his portrait provided an insight into its currency and intensity of authority [Figure 11]. Mugabe's official portrait was a stilted image, bereft of any signs of ease of leadership and power. In his dark suit and large spectacles, he stares vacantly, conventionally. His face is positioned front on, making it impossible to avoid his gaze.

Once Mugabe's resignation became clear, it was at his portrait that the first orders were directed: the managing director of Zimbabwean telecommunications company TelOne instructed all company stations to immediately take it down. Rubbish bins overflowed with his picture, now the detritus of his regime. In London, the Zimbabwe Human Rights Organisation removed Mugabe's portrait from the Embassy, attacked it, then burnt it in the street – a sign of the eradication of the dictator from their lives.

Mugabe governed by outmoded policy and fear, supported by those complicit in his programs, and the display of his portrait had provided security in a regime that demanded loyalty. In June 2017, for example, Obadiah Musindo, founder of Destiny for Afrika and supporter of Mugabe's ZANU–PF ruling party, highlighted the powerful role of the dictator's portrait to the beneficiaries of his low-income housing scheme for Zimbabweans:

Our people would be very soon receiving title deeds. I am happy now that our people know our conditions for joining our projects. We don't threaten people, but they should know that we also have our conditions . . . Those portraits [of Mugabe] should not be hidden in bedrooms, but should be in open spaces. We are going to set small groups in communities, where people will spy on each other because our houses belong only to Zanu PF supporters.[23]

In the final days of Mugabe's leadership, Musindo remained strong in his support and continued his forthright proclamations regarding Mugabe's portrait. In his directions about voter registration, for example, he stated:

If you fail to bring proof that you have registered we are going to expel you from our stands or we charge you commercial rates. Put simply, we will expel because when you registered to be our member we gave you cards with President Robert Mugabe's portrait on it, so you need to follow our teachings.[24]

Musindo placed a great deal of importance on those cards – they were a daily reminder to beneficiaries of their debt and of whom they had to follow. It is, of course, horrible abuse of those who had the least power and freedom of choice. There was no escape from Mugabe's portrait. It was in every office building, in every hotel lobby.

Portraits of a former leader authenticate the past. Objectors to the destruction of Mugabe's portrait cited the need to preserve the historical evidence – arguing that to erase the portrait erased a significant component of thirty years of rule. Yet as each dictator is deposed, people's anger and violent response to the oppression focuses on the portraits. The portraits of Colonel Gaddafi, Saddam Hussein and Ferdinand Marcos were targeted as a sign of freedom from the brutality of their rule.

There is purpose in searching the face of someone such as Mugabe, whom you could never know, trying to find within it a clue to the mind and behaviour of a dictator. As philosopher Michel Foucault put it:

> . . . it is already one of the prime effects of power that certain bodies, certain gestures, certain discourses, certain desires, come to be identified and constituted as individuals.[25]

CHAPTER 4

Royalty
and
Nobility

Portraits of royalty and the nobility are destroyed all the time. While
we might imagine that the image of the aristocrat is protected for
posterity, the destruction is often swift and resolute. The role of
a noble and titled person varies throughout the continents, yet
fundamentally the honour is derived from a system designed to
separate class and protect legacy.

The nobility within British and European society habitually
exists as one step below royalty and, like royalty, the beneficiaries
are usually born into positions of power. Royal families enjoy the
luxury of continuity of power through the birth of the first child.
Absolute monarchies whereby the head of the family also exercises
executive powers are rare. Most royal families are designated as
constitutional and provide a ceremonial role in state affairs, with the
families living courtesy of the grace and favour of the state. Royalty,

as such, has little relevance to contemporary life for the majority of world citizens, although it defines for some a historical lineage and a sense of comfort in the continuity that royalty affords. Hereditary power can extend to some parliamentary structures as in Britain, which retains ninety-two hereditary peerages in its House of Lords, peerages passing to male offspring in the first instance.

Entitled and elitist, one group succours the other, ensuring the impenetrable coterie retains a separate social status and influence – and continues to inherit considerable wealth, often dominating the potential for the entire population of a nation to prosper. In Britain, one third of the land remains under aristocratic ownership. As historian Chris Bryant puts it:

> they seized it by conquest, they expropriated it from the monasteries and they enclosed it for their private use under the pretence of efficiency. They grasped wealth, corruptly carved out their niche at the pinnacle of society and held on to it with a vice-like grip.[1]

The Reformation in Europe saw to the destruction of statues and images of idolatry in the churches, and when it arrived in England there was a similar clearing in keeping with the Protestant aesthetic. A clearing of possessions also occurred for those marched off to the gallows; Sir Thomas More and Sir Thomas Cromwell were victims of the removal of their belongings along with their heads. Prior to their demise, they were fortunate to be the subjects of magnificent portraits by Hans Holbein the Younger. A portrait of Cromwell attributed to Holbein is now in New York's Frick Collection, but

Tudor historian Roy Strong is not satisfied that the contemplative, exacting commissioned portrait painted from life by Holbein actually survived the collection of goods by the Crown. Strong's analysis proposes that the Frick painting credited to Holbein is the best of the three early versions of the portrait that exist. Certainly, the Frick gallery is of the view that it is an original and that there is enough evidence to conclude it to be a portrait by Holbein.[2] While it did happen that belongings were destroyed along with the declared treasonous individuals, the belongings were more likely to be sold as had occurred with religious assets in order to assist with funding the campaigns and extravagances of the Crown.

Fortunately for the legacy of British art, there wasn't a rebellious campaign that included the widespread destruction of portraiture of the ruling class in the same manner as had occurred in France. Following the formation of the Paris Commune in 1792 during the French Revolution, statues of the former kings including Henry IV and Louis XIII, XIV and XV were smashed to the ground in an effort to erase the historical legacy of entitlement and autocratic monarchy. Revolutionary politics sanctioned the activities while the contemporary radical publications observed that:

> for those who cannot read, it will be as though these names and ceremonies had never existed. We should speak to the people of their glory by means of a public monument.[3]

Paintings were not exempt from such wreckage. In the days following the storming of the Bastille, bonfires were fuelled with pictures of the royal and noble ruling classes, wildly dragged from the chateaux by bands of revolutionaries as though they were dragging the actual persons from their beds to be executed. This was the fate of one of a number of portraits of Louis XIII by Philippe de Champaigne; apparently the work was almost saved due to its artistic value but was ultimately thrown into the fire anyway to be burnt as a sign that the era of past 'despotism' was gone.[4] The destruction of the past was sanctioned, as Stanley Idzerda has investigated, by the council of the Paris Commune in spite of the advice of the Monuments Commission instigated to protect works of artistic merit during the unrest.

Many of the new order were in favour of the complete eradication of any signs of the former ruling class, although concerns that France would be considered by the rest of the world a country of barbaric iconoclasts, as well as one that had disintegrated into a cultural desert, were an issue. Extraordinarily, the Neo-Classical painter Jacques-Louis David supported the bonfires and pillaging, and proposed a bronze statue on the Pont Neuf to counter the idolatry of the past. The statue would be designed for the people and cast from the remnants of the destroyed statues of the kings – such was David's anger towards the principles of the monarchy.[5] David was a powerful political figure during the Revolution (and the subsequent Reign of Terror) having personally signed the death warrants for King Louis XVI, Marie Antoinette and many others who he believed posed a danger to the cause of the people.

Destruction and revolution are extreme measures, yet, in this case, resulted in a modern and liberal program of change. The eighteenth century was the Age of Enlightenment, a philosophical approach that embraced independent thought and increased political and cultural autonomy. Emerging from the destruction of the Revolution was the designation of a wing of the Louvre Palace as a national museum. It was a refuge for those works considered to be of artistic merit and, therefore, worthy of protection, literally rescuing an artistic legacy from the hands of the revolutionaries. The Louvre Palace had been a fortress of display of the majesty of French royalty and housed the Royal Academy of Painting and Sculpture. Established in 1648, the once-impenetrable Academy was absorbed into the people's Musée Central des Arts, a product of the Revolution. It embraced the new approach to the notion of art; no longer a facility for the imaging of royal-sanctioned practice and display, it could exist as an entity unto itself.

For years David, other artists and even Louis XVI's appointed Director General, Comte d'Angiviller, had championed for the doors of the Academy to be opened to the public. D'Angiviller had commissioned historical works in an effort to increase patriotism but, of course, that was to no avail if the public could not view them. The Luxembourg Gallery in Paris had been open for six hours per week, but this was clearly not enough to satisfy the needs of the French public and travellers. The Musée Central in the Louvre Palace opened its doors on 10 August 1793, one year after the fall of the monarchy and timed to coincide with David's Festival of Fraternity, a procession through the streets of Paris to celebrate victory for the people and salute the new symbols of France.

Of course, the French were not the first to take issue with the monarchy and nobility. A document written by Abbé Grégoire in 1794 responded to the vandalism (a word he invented) in France and he made an urgent plea for the destruction to end, reminding the French people of the downfall of the Roman Empire. The Romans willingly destroyed statues and portraits of deposed emperors and their families along with the associated discourse. Statues were smashed as a sign that a reign had passed; the sadly mutilated face thought to be of Emperor Macrinus [Figure 12] was damaged after he was deposed following only eighteen months of rule.[6] The speed with which leaders were replaced and often killed during the Roman period meant that time, and sometimes skill, was in short supply when a new statue was required. A new leader might have to do with the transformation of a plaster portrait of the previous leader. The destruction of a portrait symbolised allegiance to a new leader; reconfiguring of an old image or statue was a sustainable means of compliance with a regime change.

Portraiture of the Imperial Roman women was just as susceptible to destruction and is pivotal to the narrative of their varying fortunes and survival. Women exiled without an allowance were left to starve to death, babies were 'exposed' to die under emperors' orders, bodies were dismembered and thrown over cliffs, and forced suicides and poisonings awaited many of the women who flirted with imperial power. In 2 BCE it was Julia, the wife of Tiberius and daughter of

Augustus, who was banished for adultery, the condemnation of her life beginning with the destruction of her portraits. Given her lineage there would have been a substantial portrait legacy, but, as concluded by Eric Varner, most were destroyed or warehoused, with coin images and inconclusive likenesses all that remain.[7]

Agrippina Major [Figure 13], born in 14 BCE, publicly challenged her uncle Tiberius, which effectively sealed her fate and the destiny of some of her nine children. As granddaughter of Augustus and the widow of Germanicus, she held a certain power within Roman society, but her desire to remarry set her on a path of opposition with Tiberius. He managed to convince the Senate to have her exiled, but not before portraits of Agrippina were carried by her followers throughout the streets as a sign of support. The portraits could not save her, however, and it was during her exile that she starved herself to death. When her son, Caligula, became emperor one of his first public acts was to retrieve her ashes and produce representations of her for posterity.

Portraits then, as now, were a political tool, a contested site of allegiance. For some, the power of representation remains. Most recently, ISIS was responsible for the smashing of statues that are a part of the heritage of the Syrian town of Palmyra, once a thriving, wealthy metropolis belonging to the Roman Empire until rebellion struck. The keeper of Palmyra's antiquities, Khaled al-Asaad, chose to be beheaded rather than divulge the whereabouts of the precious heritage, much of which he had managed to move to a safe refuge. The Palmyrene funerary busts were among the works destroyed in the attacks, and while they typically didn't present accurate likenesses of their subjects, the busts provided the opportunity to study representation of the human face in the first century CE.

Ancient Egyptian hierarchy also placed considerable authority in the portrait and, equally, in its destruction as a sign of the succession of power. Famously, the portrait statues of Queen Hatshepsut in her mortuary temple at Deir el-Bahri [Figure 14] were destroyed, dumped or defaced after her death (thought to be 1458 BCE) by her successor and stepson, Thutmose III. Hatshepsut had married Thutmose II, both progeny of Thutmose I, but with Hatshepsut unable to have more children after the birth of her daughter, Thutmose II was provided an heir – Thutmose III – by a secondary wife. Hatshepsut became co-regent with Thutmose III but then assumed for herself the role of pharaoh, the female king. A number of surviving portraits of the Queen, most reconstructed after their smashing, depict her as a male pharaoh in keeping with her authority as the holder of the office, wearing the official regalia of the Khat on her head as well as the false beard.

Following her death, Thutmose III ordered all of her statues to be removed from the temple of the pharaoh and destroyed in order to eradicate the memory of her rule. As Peter Dorman has indicated:

> the systematic erasure of Hatshepsut's name and figure from her kingly monuments some years after her death has, inevitably, become a lens through which historians have viewed the events of her life and reign.[8]

In addition to the destruction of statues, the raised representations of Hatshepsut were scratched, roughened, smoothed and covered with plaster, cut out and replaced until most of the images and naming of her as pharaoh were erased. It is now considered that rather than personal hatred of a stepson for his mother, Thutmose III was motivated by jealousy of the considerable importance and impact Hatshepsut had made upon her country. There is also the more likely reason that Thutmose III needed to ensure his lineage through the male. There was a very likely risk of power diverting to the many daughters with competing rights to the kingship.

What is of interest in the theories associated with the destruction is that researchers have discovered that the statues of Queen Hatshepsut produced prior to her adoption of the position of pharaoh were not attacked. Dorman suggests that it may simply be that the 'invented phenomena of the female king had created such conceptual and practical complications that the evidence of it was best erased'.[9] The erasure of the record of her contribution as leader was almost accomplished until some persistent nineteenth-century researchers translated the remnant texts that chronicled her as female king.

The portrait was evidence of rule and power – never more so than in the Renaissance period courtesy of the Medici family. They employed it to substantiate legitimacy of rule, and a legacy of exquisite portraits by Italian masters unfold throughout the fifteenth and sixteenth centuries, validating the reigning heads of the Medici family in

Florence. With the emergence of Cosimo i de' Medici, Grand Duke of Tuscany, in the sixteenth century, the battle between legitimate male heirs from multiple family lineages required substantial creativity to both protect and secure claims to the head of the Florentine ducal title.

Multiples of portraits of the Medici family were painted and distributed to friends and enemies to remind them not only of who was in power but also the means by which the lineage of that power was to unfold. This is the period of the matriarchal portrait in Florentine art – the mother posed with her child, the heir to the ducal title. The *Portrait of Eleonora di Toledo with her son Giovanni* (1545; Uffizi Gallery, Florence) by Bronzino, the court painter to the Medici family, is a flawless example of this tradition. Eleonora was Cosimo's wife; Giovanni was her fourth son, his destiny to be sanctioned as a Cardinal at the age of seventeen. The splendid couture of Eleonora, who bore Cosimo eleven children before her early death at forty, and the solemnity of the Uffizi portrait are evidence of the importance of the matriarchal portrait as a document of power.

During the two centuries of rule of the Medici family, all heirs (other than three of the Medici heirs apparent) had their portraits painted with their mother, the end of the Medici dynasty somewhat marking the end of this tradition. Eleonora's son Francesco went on to succeed his father by becoming the Grand Duke of Tuscany and marrying Joanna of Austria, with whom he had six daughters and one son, Filippo. However, Francesco also had an affair with Bianca Cappello, who bore him a son, Antonio, prior to the birth of Filippo in 1577. When Joanna died in 1578, Francesco installed Bianca as his wife – although, of course, Filippo was still heir. In 1581 Alessandro Allori painted a triple portrait of Bianca with Filippo and Antonio. The work signified an extraordinary coup on her part to have her portrait painted with the heir apparent and, should anything happen to Filippo, an illegitimate heir apparent as the half-brother to the future Grand Duke.

The mother and her two sons all wore white silk for the portrait as an obvious sign of purity and legitimacy. The portrait was copied and sent to descendants of the Medici patriarchy as well as those with whom strategic alliances were to be formed. It was a sign of the strength of the marriage and the lineage. Unfortunately, Filippo died one year after the painting of the portrait, resulting in Francesco having to convince the Medici family of Antonio as heir. It was to no avail. Francesco and Bianca died – either, it is believed, through poisoning or malaria – in 1587 and Ferdinando, Francesco's brother, stepped in, denied Antonio as legitimate heir and assumed the title. Having hated Bianca, he also ensured that she was not to be remembered in any honorific manner.

It almost goes without saying that one of the best ways to destroy support for a potential heir is to destroy the record and surety of that lineage by destroying any portraits in existence. Antonio probably counted himself lucky to make it out of the battle for power alive. Between the years 1537 and 1560, Cosimo, his grandfather, had ordered the grisly public execution of twenty-two of his opponents. Art historian Heather Holian has researched the fate of the triple portrait plus other portraits that documented Bianca's nine years as ducal wife.[10] Not only is the original triple portrait missing, but no copies of the work remain. Apparently, Ferdinando ordered the destruction of everything – including portraits, coats-of-arms and inscriptions – that would link Bianca and her heir to the Medicis and remind people of her position. It was not, as Holian remarks, a complete *damnatio memoriae*, and portraits of Bianca alone or with Antonio still exist [Figure 15]. The triple portrait could have proved fatal to Ferdinando should it be used as evidence of Antonio's legitimacy to the Grand Ducal position. Destruction of the portrait was the only recourse to ensure his prosperity and power.

In Britain, it was during the Tudor period that portraiture gained currency, and images of the faces of royal households were often copied multiple times to be distributed as propaganda. Of course, by presenting the portrait in that context, it was more often than not destined to be destroyed along with the ruler.

Without doubt the most famous face of a reigning monarch would have to be the richly auburn, bountiful, gilded and adorned King Henry VIII, the portrait images by Hans Holbein the Younger, the German artist who became the King's official painter in 1535, creating the popular version. Holbein revelled in the opulence of the King's regal trappings, a typical portrayal being the life-size 1537 mural of Henry, his parents and Queen Jane Seymour, his third wife, that adorned Whitehall Palace until a fire destroyed the vast residence of the royal family in 1698. Fortuitously, thirty years prior to the fire, the artist Remigius van Leemput undertook a copy of the mural that now resides in the Royal Collection and provides a record of the substantial work. The multiple portraits document the meaning of power in Henry's court, with power embodied in the stance of Henry VIII, his ivory legs determinedly astride, his cumbersome frame almost the size of the three members of his family combined. Art historian Shearer West concludes that:

> [the] hierarchic painting therefore serves a dynastic purpose – to glorify the House of Tudor and to hint at the continuation of the line through the representation of two generations of the Tudors.[11]

There are copies of the mural portrait of Henry VIII that distil the likeness and intensity of his force, one of these attributed to Holbein, others to his workshop, still others to sixteenth-century artists. It is courtesy of the magnificent portrait in the Palazzo Barberini collection in Rome that we understand the meaning of power as invested in Henry VIII along with his uncompromising authority and barbaric treatment of most of his six wives. The wide, fur-encumbered, rose-and-gold-filigreed shoulders fill the width of the picture frame, while his stout chest carries the weight of gilded adornments. In spite of all of this, it is the dark, hazel, watchful eyes, arched eyebrows and small cinched mouth that create the sense of fear and foreboding. To gaze into the eyes that watched, scrutinised and besought his poor suffering wives is to begin to understand the notion of abuse and fear. His wives were sought for their ability to produce an heir to the throne. They were generally people born without the skills to manipulate his authority, and their means of survival was to cower to his might and his unbending need for stature and longevity through the male line.

The reign of Henry VIII according to the noted Tudor historian Roy Strong 'witnesses the birth of modern royal portraiture and sets the pace for the next 300 years'.[12] There was a 'vast increase' in royal portraiture, linked of course to the Reformation and the destruction of Catholic images of idolatry, with possession of a royal portrait 'a symbol of loyalty to the Crown in troubled times'. Those portraits, however, were not necessarily symbols of survival.

The Tudor reign dominated by Henry VIII and his ancestors is littered with examples of portraits destroyed as he dispensed with wives, advisers and apparent adulterers. Catherine of Aragon, the first wife, to whom Henry was married for almost twenty-four years, did not produce a male heir to the throne – her only surviving child a daughter, Mary, who eventually became Queen Mary I. As a result of this apparent failure, Henry chose to seek an annulment to the marriage, which led to the rift with the Pope, the Protestant Reformation and the establishment of the Church of England, but he refused to send his wife to the gallows. Other wives followed: Anne Boleyn, mother to Queen Elizabeth I (although again the marriage was annulled, but this time Henry's ex-wife was beheaded); Jane Seymour became his third wife thirteen days after the beheading but died shortly after the birth of her son, later crowned as Edward VI; Anne of Cleves for six months (she managed to survive); Catherine Howard for a year, but she was also executed; and finally, Catherine (Kateryn) Parr in 1543 until Henry's death some three years later.

To enter the world of portraiture of the wives of Henry VIII is to be presented with interpretations of evidence as varied as the symbols that populate the oeuvre, and a body of work that was often much altered, annotated and misattributed – usually for the political and social gain of the owner.

A comparison of all of Henry VIII's wives shows that they had quite similar features; they were usually fair with dark eyes and were very young when they married – this attribute alone equating with beauty throughout the centuries. Most recently, a portrait in the Lambeth Palace collection originally thought to be a young Catherine Parr was identified as Catherine of Aragon [Figure 16]. Black paint had covered the veil and the patterned background, while the subject's nose had been narrowed and the eyebrows and lips darkened. The original pose of a half-turned face, demure and compliant, hands cupped protectively towards her body in a maternal manner, remained. What is most interesting about the discovery of the two portraits by the National Portrait Gallery conservators was their assessment that the original portrait had been deliberately damaged with scathes on the face causing paint loss.[13] This may be evidence of anger towards the devoutly Catholic Catherine of Aragon or an attempt to scrape the paint in order to prepare the surface for a newly renovated portrait of Catherine Parr.

A portrait should have been, in sixteenth-century England, true to life, thus evoking the spirit of the person and their beliefs. The original portrait of Catherine of Aragon had been a companion piece to a more demure and younger, slimmer Henry than the one we are used to. Catherine of Aragon had refused to denounce her religion or step aside and accommodate Henry's desire for an annulment. There were many who saw Catherine as the enemy, while others were angry at her obstinacy that wrought the new religion. There were burnings of Lutherans and Catholics who did not abide by Henry's rule. Anger in the form of a physical attack upon the original portrait is not out of the question. Equally, overpainting was a common occurrence in the Tudor period, with many works receiving multiple attempts at either improving the image on the panel or a complete covering and new portrait.[14]

Henry did not usually roam too far for each subsequent wife. Some had played roles as lady-in-waiting (Jane Seymour, Catherine Howard, Catherine Parr); Anne Boleyn was sister to one of Henry's mistresses; and others had been sought for their dowries and strategic connections to European royalty. It was following the death of Jane Seymour that Henry realised he had not groomed a replacement wife and needed to find a suitable choice, preferably someone with a European title. Distance and a reliance upon sixteenth-century transport made the search rather difficult, especially if you are the King of England. To assist with the King's quest for a beautiful, connected, non-Catholic wife, Holbein was dispatched to paint the portraits of prospective brides. It was, if you will, a long-form version of online dating.

Henry's father, Henry VII, had previously undertaken a similar enterprise in reverse. He had sent a portrait upon its way at the behest of Herman Rinck, who was attempting to negotiate a union between Henry VII and the French-educated and recently widowed Margaret, Duchess of Savoy, who was the daughter of Maximilian I, Holy Roman Emperor. Yet Margaret was distraught at her husband's death, had attempted suicide from a window and vowed never to marry again. It is hard to imagine the forthright Margaret, who became Governor of the Low Countries (predominantly Belgium and Netherlands), showing an interest in the slightly pernicious image of Henry VII that arrived to convince her of marriage. The 1505 portrait, by an unknown Netherlandish artist, is now held in the National Portrait Gallery, London. It is a perfect counterpoint to the unbounded authority of the Holbein portrait of Henry VIII.

Holbein returned from his travels to Europe in 1538 and 1539 with at least three portraits for Henry VIII. He produced within a three-hour sitting a full-length portrait of the widow Christina of Denmark, Duchess of Milan, dressed in her fur-lined black widow's coat. He also returned with two miniatures of the sisters Amelia (Amalia) and Anne of Cleves from the northern Rhineland. It is understood that Henry looked at the two Cleves portraits and decided upon Anne; the miniature can be found in the Victoria and Albert Museum, while a compact half-portrait rendering of Anne by Holbein is in the Musée du Louvre.

The half-portrait of Anne presents her as introspective, with her clasped hands covering her womb and raising the expectations of children. Her gaze is not directed at the viewer but, instead, distantly contemplates her future. Henry chose well if it was friendship that he was in need of. While the marriage did not last, Anne remained within his court and became known as 'the King's sister', and had treasures and houses bestowed upon her until her early death at forty-one. The miniature portrait of Amelia is lost, but given Henry's age and urgency for a suitable male heir, it is most likely that there were other portraits presented to him that are now lacking identification, were painted over, or were – of course – destroyed. A queen does not need reminders of other beauties, nor does a king need to be prompted of another he should have chosen.

Henry VIII chose his wives according to his desire to efficiently pass on the crown to his direct bloodline, and a young woman is more likely to assist with that process. He was also attracted to a type, and in spite of reports that Henry considered Anne of Cleves to be not quite as handsome as her portrait had anticipated, Holbein losing favour with Henry as a result, he considered her suitably within the style of his bride. Henry was not interested in difference; he desired order and mimicry within his court, feeling more comfortable with an image of a wife he could understand. This sameness extended to his own likeness: he wore a beard and, having brought it back into fashion, ordered all about his court to wear one, too.

In spite of Henry VIII's best efforts, his male heir as successor was not secured. Edward VI was crowned King at the age of nine but died six years later in 1553 from illness, having governed under the stewardship of a Privy Council. He did, however, manage to exhibit a determined view on the royal succession and decided upon Lady

Jane Grey, great-granddaughter of Henry VII and grandniece of Henry VIII, to assume the throne.

Edward's choice of successor meant that he ignored the birth rights of his half-sisters Mary and Elizabeth, whom he had declared as illegitimate, a declaration that naturally did not sit well with Mary or the King's advisors, who scrambled to shore up their positions following the untimely death. An elaborate and complex game of allegiances had been set in motion years earlier by Henry's Third Succession Act of 1544, which made it possible to challenge Edward's choice. Lady Jane was Queen for only nine days, after which she was manoeuvred out of position by Mary and her supporters. Mary was proclaimed as Queen – she became known as Bloody Mary – and with her youthful insecurities mixed with her upbringing in Henry's court, spoiled further by seditious plots whispered in her ears, she gave into her fears and had Lady Jane moved to the gaol in the Tower of London. Lady Jane's fate had quickly changed from awaiting her coronation in the apartments in the Tower on 10 July 1553, to standing trial in November that year, to the execution of her and her husband, Lord Dudley, on 12 February 1554. Lady Jane was approximately seventeen years old when she died.

It is remarkable that no confirmed portrait taken from life of Lady Jane Grey exists today other than possibly as a miniature held in the Yale Center for British Art – although the claim for the identity of the woman as Lady Jane has been disputed.[15] She had significant connections to the royal household prior to her declaration as Queen and would have had a portrait completed while she awaited her coronation. The portrait was an important instrument in exhibiting authority to the people. Lady Jane needed to display her governing mandate to Mary, who was increasingly emboldened by the seeming alacrity with which she was able to amass support in the days following the death of Edward. Portraits would have also been employed to display Lady Jane's beauty, an attribute that could inspire devotion and allegiance. There is no doubt that the execution of Lady Jane was accompanied by the destruction of any portraits in process – or they were quickly painted over with a portrait of the new Queen Mary I.

Queen Elizabeth I's ascension to the throne followed the death of Mary I in 1559. In spite of a brief period during which she had been incarcerated in the Tower of London on charges of supporting Protestantism in opposition to Mary's devout Catholicism, she had generally received support from her half-sister. Elizabeth formed the English Protestant Church, was forthright in declaring her love for her people, refused to respond positively to any courtships by prospective suitors and proclaimed she was wedded to her subjects. Her faith and commitment were returned with affection by her people, who desired to own a portrait of the Queen.

Always ready to enhance her reputation, in 1563 Elizabeth drafted a proposal whereby 'some speciall person that shall be by hir allowed' would have control and approval over finished portraits, after which others would be able to copy that image.[16] Demands for the portraits were received from across England – and beyond. The desire for her portrait was further enhanced in 1570 when the Pope declared that he had excommunicated Queen Elizabeth I from the Catholic Church. In response, the display of her portrait became a popular expression of loyalty.

The historian Elizabeth Pomeroy has estimated that there remains in existence some hundred and thirty-five painted portraits of Elizabeth, although they are survivors of a much greater number.[17] There were many portraits that caused the Queen much consternation and, as a result, orders to control the portraiture were made by the Queen's Privy Council. It was important for her people, she decreed, to have a picture that conveyed her regal beauty, that could be gazed upon and inspire allegiance to her Crown and to her Protestant religion and no other. Debased portraits that caused great offence either through their lack of likeness to the Queen or deficiency in regal quality had to be destroyed, with many, according to the testimony of Sir Walter Raleigh, cast into lustrous bonfires.[18] Elizabeth was known for her feats of war, reducing and destroying armies and would-be conquerors, and to complement that she constructed an official image that was strong, commanding and, at times, beautiful.

Queen Elizabeth I's portraits evolved into what became known as supporting the 'mask of youth', portraits that effectively hid her ageing appearance; to hint at such weakness could be detrimental to the safety of the country. Elizabeth would not appear in court until her ladies had wigged and gowned and masked her with the toxic cosmetics that were available. To be privy to the unadorned image of Elizabeth was to risk incarceration – as Robert Devereux, the Earl of

Essex, discovered. He had angrily burst into Elizabeth's bedchamber one morning in 1599 and for his brashness was later confined to his rooms. It placed the Earl in conflict with his Queen, and it is tempting to speculate that the incident had sown the seeds for his eventual execution a couple of years later due to a poor campaign in Ireland and the raising of a contingent to overthrow Elizabeth.

With time of the essence and the painting process never quick, artists were often required to paint a portrait of the Queen over an older portrait – that may or may not have been of Elizabeth – or to adjust a portrait for greater clarity of message. One such example, *Queen Elizabeth I* (1580s–1590s; National Portrait Gallery, London), has both the portrait of another subject beneath Elizabeth's portrait and shows evidence of changes to accommodate the wishes of Elizabeth's 'speciall person'. Over time, deteriorating transparent paints have gradually revealed the face of an unknown original sitter beneath the portrait of the Queen. X-radiography analysis has also shown that Elizabeth's portrait underwent a number of changes. Elizabeth holds a serpent in the underpainting of her portrait, the overpainting of a bouquet of flowers most likely ordered to counter the conflicting meanings of the serpent, which vary from connoting Satan to a sign of reasoning.[19] Part of the serpent that twines through and around her fingers is now visible beneath the paint loss.

Elizabeth's reign was secured with the defeat of the Spanish Armada in 1588, and it is in the grand commemorative portraits that it is possible to discern the measure of her power and regal stature. Yet the three portraits that became known as the Armada portraits of Elizabeth did not escape modification over the years. The portrait in the National Portrait Gallery, *Queen Elizabeth I*, c.1588, by an unknown artist, documents subtle changes to the Queen's appearance. The portrait was cut down on all sides (which may have occurred much later) and the seascapes in the background were only revealed after conservation work. An x-radiograph shows that Elizabeth was originally painted with a softer face, and her fabulous red curls were left unkempt, giving her an appearance that suggests her humanity rather than her authority.[20] It is a difficult assessment for conservators – to change a portrait back or accept the changes as they have been made. For another of the Armada portraits that now resides in the Greenwich Museum, the choice has been made to leave two scenes of the Armada ships that were added early in the eighteenth century. The assessment is that the public is now used to seeing the portrait in this state, and to remove them would disrupt the familiarity of engagement.

Elizabeth asserted her subjectivity in a fundamentally patriarchal society. Yet self-definition was not uncommon among British aristocratic women in the sixteenth century, as Barbara Harris has determined, particularly when there were fortunes and titles to protect and pass onto sons.[21] Portraits of women with their sons were common as a statement of lineage. Elizabeth bore no children and had to tread a fine line between supporting her close relatives and simultaneously ensuring they did not covet the throne before she was ready to leave it.

Elizabeth attached to her waist a small ruby-jewelled case to keep miniature portraits of those she cared about close to her. In 1566 the Spanish Ambassador observed Elizabeth carrying a portrait of Mary I of Scotland (Mary Queen of Scots) – her cousin first removed. It was the same Queen whose execution Elizabeth ordered twenty-one years later due to treason.[22] As she was confined for nineteen years prior to the execution, portraits of Mary Queen of Scots, the Catholic Queen of Scotland, taken from life, are very few in number.

Elizabeth followed in her father's footsteps, incarcerating, beheading and banishing those guilty of conspiracy against her, considered as credible threats to her reign or followers of Catholicism – or all of the above! Mary's grandmother had been Henry VIII's sister. Mary was imprisoned initially in Scotland for ill-advised choices in husbands (it was believed her third husband, the Protestant James Hepburn, fourth Earl of Bothwell, had been involved in the assassination of her second Catholic husband Henry Stewart, Earl of Darnley, who, in turn, had been accused of killing Mary's apparent lover), but after she fled to England it was her political threat to Elizabeth that sealed her fate.

Mary saw her infant son James for the last time in April 1567 as she took flight in order to preserve her life, leaving him with the Earl and Countess of Mar; her abdication resulted in his crowning at only one year of age. The story has been told many times, but what is of interest in this reading is the impact of such activities upon the lack of a legacy of portraiture of a woman for whom, given her birthright, her elevation to Queen of France following her first marriage to François II, declarations of her as the Queen of England and

Scotland, we would expect a substantial visual record. Unfortunately, there are very few confirmed portraits from life of Mary that are extant [Figure 17].

Elizabeth, a woman intently obsessed with her image and its impact, employed it to force loyalty and remind her subjects of her position as the Queen. Mary posed a threat to her reign and, following the inconclusive inquiry into the murder of Darnley by Mary, Elizabeth chose to confine Mary in the opulent surroundings at Hardwick Hall under the guard of the Earl of Shrewsbury. With Mary's confinement, Scotland was relatively stable in the late sixteenth century under the static court of James VI, yet her corporal existence disturbed some of Elizabeth's ministers who, eager to be rid of the threat Mary posed to the English Crown and Protestant control, would excite Elizabeth with their plots and rumours. Eventually, Mary was accused of treason against Elizabeth and was then executed.

The lack of verified portraits of Mary can be attributed to her having spent nearly half her life incarcerated, although there were opportunities for portraits to be painted. In addition, from age six to nineteen, she resided in France as the betrothed to the Dauphin of France. He would become King François II, and they married when Mary was just fifteen. Nineteenth-century historian Lionel Cust has observed that it is barely credible that no portraits save some drawings exist from this time of the young Queen of France, the loss of the works no doubt subject to the turmoil of the houses and perhaps the life of the Queen who, following the death of her young French husband, returned to Scotland in 1561. Cust has written of the general confusion over her portraiture, the attempts by many to claim portraits as those of the Queen, no matter that the women in the pictures had an array of hair and eye colours that differed markedly from her red-gold tresses and dark hazel eyes.

Importantly, the verified portraits of Mary are those that remained in the possession of her family and her gaolers, the Earl and Countess of Shrewsbury, and were bequeathed into significant collections as a result of these connections. It must be said that there were very few portrait artists circulating in Scotland at the time, and there was an apparent subdued interest in portraiture in comparison with Elizabeth's court. According to the Scottish Treasurer's accounts, there were no commissioned portraits of Mary by her household even though there are painted portraits from this time – perhaps any portraits were gifts of the artist.[23] Mary was considered to have run a court of luxury, with opulent furnishings and art, but perhaps, unlike Elizabeth, she saw no currency in the distribution of her portrait – or many of her portraits were destroyed.

There are also very few verifiable portraits of Darnley in spite of his position as King of Scotland following his marriage to Mary. In 1926 Karl Pearson undertook an analysis of Darnley's skull, robbed from his tomb in the seventeenth century, assessing its structure and compliance with apparent portraits of the King. It was an extraordinary exercise in which he also analysed the myriad documents that survive to both condemn and exonerate Mary. He lambasted the vitriol and plotting against the Queen by those he referred to as the Scottish Tuchans, who, he noted, nearly all met untimely deaths for their sins. Their power and hatred of Catholicism led to behaviour that Pearson summarises as: 'they bled their country, destroyed its ancient monuments, blasted the life of the Queen'.[24] It is behaviour consistent with the few portraits that have survived and testimony of a destructive attitude.

The lack of response by the Scottish public to seek a rescue of their Queen, being party to the stories of their Queen's conspiracy to murder one husband and to engage in an affair while still married, is also consistent with the ambivalent response of James VI to the incarceration of his mother:

> How fond and inconstant I were if I should prefer my mother to the title, let all men judge. My religion ever moved me to hate her course, although my honour constrains me to insist for her life.[25]

It can be speculated that if portraits from life had been available to the King, portraits upon which he could gaze and consider the maternal, the sincerity of his mother's feelings for him – a portrait that displayed the texture of her skin, the strong aquiline nose as though it had just breathed the air – could he have allowed her death to take place? The famous *En Deuil Blanc* (*White Mourning*) drawing by François Clouet, as discussed by Forrest P. Chisman, is the one picture from life that presents Mary in a moment of contemplation, yet this singular picture remained in France following her return to Scotland. As Chisman writes, if a portrait 'demonstrates nothing else, it is the lasting power of a good image. Clouet's drawing is deeply personal'.[26]

Mary Queen of Scots yearned for her young son throughout her exile and confinement. He was tutored by Protestants, her gifts to him were not delivered and letters in which she begged for her freedom were not handed to her son. James' first letter to his mother was written as late as March 1585 when he was eighteen – it must have been a long time for a mother to wait to hear from her son. She had kept beside her a thin gold case with a folding flap, described in her probate inventory as 'a book of gold enamelled [and] containing the pictures of the late Scottish Queen, her husband and her son', among other portraits she managed to smuggle out of Scotland.[27]

However, Mary clearly felt the need for a portrait that showed her son as adult king, and in 1585 she wrote to M. D'Esneval, the French Ambassador in Edinburgh, to ask him to obtain a portrait of her son 'drawn from his own person'. D'Esneval organised a portrait to be copied from another portrait which, of course, was not her intention. He maintained that the King was 'greatly obliged by this mark of affection'.[28] The court painter Adrian Vanson had completed a portrait of James VI in 1585 to hang in Edinburgh Castle, and it may be a copy of that portrait that was sent to James' exiled mother.

It is clear that Elizabeth equivocated over executing the Catholic Scottish Queen, not, it would seem, out of kindness, but because world opinion was not in sympathy with her confinement of Mary.

It prompted Elizabeth's 'reluctance to stand forth to the world as her acknowledged executioner'.[29] Scotland, at the time, needed the support of Elizabeth. While she had requested that Mary stop using the title of Queen, eventually she acknowledged King James VI, who would later become her successor as James I of England and Ireland. Nevertheless, Mary was executed in 1587 at Fotheringhay Castle.

The sensitivity of displaying the image of Mary after her execution is evident in a portrait possibly again by Vanson held in the National Portrait Gallery and recently discovered via x-radiography. On top of Mary's portrait lies another portrait, this one definitely by Vanson, who in 1589 chose to cover her face with a portrait of King James VI's Lord Chancellor, Sir John Maitland.

Maitland was a former supporter of Mary in the Marian Civil War that flared up following her abdication. He battled against those who ruled in the name of King James VI but, eventually reinstated, became one of the most important advisers in Scotland during the period of the portrait. When Mary Queen of Scots signed letters of abdication in 1567, her Protestant half-brother, James Stewart, 1st Earl of Moray, who had continually disparaged and fought her, was made Regent for James VI. He prevented her attempts to regain power and was subsequently assassinated in 1570. With the Marian Civil War raging through Scotland, there needed to be leadership. In the letters of abdication, it had been expressly indicated that should anything happen to Moray, a balanced council of five of the nobility was to govern. It was due to the efforts of Maitland's brother, William Maitland, and his compatriot William Kirkcaldy, both former opponents of Mary but supporters during the war, that the council was formed to support James VI as King. They both died, one in prison, the other hanged, at the end of the war in 1573.

James VI posthumously reinstated Kirkcaldy's lands to his heirs, indicative of the complexity of the political relationships in Scotland at that time but also as an acknowledgement of the blood ties between the King and his incarcerated mother. His attempts to respect and honour the efforts of those who had fought on his mother's side may have been meant as a sign to his mother of his support. He was also highly aware that Catholicism was still practised and many felt that he should take a greater stand against Elizabeth. When Mary's execution was beyond doubt, she wrote to Elizabeth that she should at least 'permit me to send a jewel and a last adieu to my son with my dying benediction, for of my blessing he has been deprived'.[30] There was no response. The news of their Queen's execution 'was received in Scotland with a burst of national indignation, so uncontrollable... insulting libels against Queen Elizabeth...were placarded on the walls of Edinburgh'.[31]

It appears from the portrait hidden beneath Maitland that images of Mary were painted, sold and presumably displayed in Scotland at the time of her death. Vanson was an accomplished portrait painter who had quickly found favour with James VI and thus became court painter in 1584. This was three years prior to the execution of Mary, three years for Vanson to have spent time with James during portrait sittings. Vanson may have taken it upon himself to paint Mary as a measure of his recognition of James' remorse, longing and sadness at a life spent without his mother. Vanson, of course, had no opportunity to observe Mary and would have relied upon the available portrait copies, coins and medals in her son's collection or those still visible in the houses of Scotland.

When Elizabeth died in 1603 and James VI became James I of England and Scotland, it was reported by the Venetian Ambassador that portraits of Elizabeth were removed and replaced with those of Mary Queen of Scots.[32] It is difficult to understand where those portraits came from – perhaps some hurriedly made copies, perhaps secretly stored portraits held by Catholic Scots who had fled to England along with their Queen many years earlier. James, out of guilt and remorse, attempted to valorise the life of his mother and commissioned a tomb in Westminster Abbey for her that was larger than the tomb for Queen Elizabeth I. He employed portraiture as a means to assist with the reinstatement of his mother's image by commissioning a number of works – perhaps as an attempt on his part to seek forgiveness for his lack of regard for her. Interestingly, many of these portraits were commissioned to show Mary as a martyr.

There remain approximately a hundred and thirty-five painted portraits of Elizabeth I, while Queen Elizabeth II has experienced (perhaps endured) the commissioning of over a hundred and fifty official portraits. From an acutely opposite approach to Elizabeth I's orders to portrait painters, Elizabeth II has bravely sat for portrait artists who run the gamut of style, skill and reverence for her position. There are some portraits that perhaps should have been destroyed; a 1953 portrait by John Napper comes to mind, while Pietro Annigoni's portraits from a similar period are remarkably haunting. Attempts have been made to destroy portraits of Elizabeth II, and most recently the portrait by Ralph Heimans was damaged with spray paint while on view at Westminster Abbey.

One of the more controversial portrait studies was painted by Lucian Freud in 2001. Sitting for a portrait by Freud, the artist for whom integrity to truth and plasticity of form was paramount, Elizabeth II was gifted a strangely enigmatic image. Famous for his protracted sitting process, Freud painted the portrait over six months, a model stepping in for the final sessions. Freud had to extend the canvas of his tiny portrait – the mesmerising and dazzling diamond diadem just couldn't be left out, the magnificent jewel eventually consuming a quarter of the space.

Like many of the portraits of Elizabeth II, the portrait was not commissioned by her but is held in the Royal Collection. The profound impact of the work is discovered in the lack of adulation by the artist for his subject. Instead, he viewed her with aged, unyielding skin that folds around her face, eyes that don't respond as warm and engaging but rather broach us with trepidation and distance.

Freud painted Elizabeth II at St James's Palace, far removed from the archaeological remnants of his paint-splattered studio, a photograph in the Royal Collection by David Dawson transmitting the intimacy of the exchange. One does not consider royalty, so usually embedded in the structuring of public image, to be secure in risking the potential of a harsh and raw imaging. There were calls for Freud to be placed in the Tower for producing such a work, and some suggested the Queen might secretly want to destroy the portrait but could not make such a public statement of vanity. While we never truly believe that people are exactly as they are portrayed in public, that all royals are always polite, mannered, kind, patient, interested and intelligent people, we also imagine that traits of a stern and bitter countenance would be quietly hidden and images tucked away.

Freud never imagined that Elizabeth II would destroy his portrait. He knew that she would recognise the signs of ageing that he, too, grappled with.

It is doubtful that when the portrait of Lady Diana Spencer by Bryan Organ went on display in the fine environment of the National Portrait Gallery three days before her wedding to Prince Charles in 1981, the artist envisaged an attempt would be made to destroy the work. The quiet, humble portrait was attacked through the centre of the picture, a bystander reporting that the 'whole of the middle was ripped out. He was still hanging onto the canvas when the security guards grabbed him'.[33]

The portrait was slashed by Paul Salmon, a student from Belfast, who proclaimed that he was in sympathy with Northern Ireland. 'I have done it for Ireland,' he stated when his charges were heard in court. His direct act of iconoclasm was upon an image for which society, at that moment, had placed one of its highest values. In the same gallery were portraits of Queen Elizabeth and Prince Charles, but they remained unscathed and were later removed from view as a precaution. Criminologists assess the attack by Salmon as the fetishisation of a portrait in which he has placed an inordinate amount of authority. Art vandalism operates in an intermediate space 'between an attack on a thing and an attack on a person', with there being a noted incidence of suicide by the perpetrator following an attack – the assault on Rembrandt's *The Night Watch* in 1975 a particular example. The act suggests a similar pattern to a real murderous action.[34]

Salmon's attack upon the portrait directly through the centre of the body of Lady Diana Spencer was akin to a disembowelling. Her innocent body, which had been thrust into a torrent of media obsession, was off-limits, but her portrait could be destroyed and his political message transmitted. The portrait, of course, was restored and remains on view today as one of the Gallery's most popular exhibits. Yet to look at the work is to remember the slashing; we cannot erase our recognition of the attack and the traversing of the portrait beyond its primary meaning.

CHAPTER 5

Why Not Mao?

The portrait of a head of government, as we have seen, is styled in a format that has currency around the world – a head and shoulders view, with the leader the only one in the picture. To be shown with partners and/or children reduces the leader's impact: they present as too homely, too much like those they are leading. Official portraits of Mao Zedong (formerly Mao Tse-tung), Chairman of the Communist Party of China from 1949 until his death in 1976, are typical examples.

Portraits of leaders are usually removed from public view once the leader is deposed, resigns or passes away. China has deviated significantly from this standard behaviour. In fact, Mao's portrait continues to be present in official settings and also, surprisingly, proliferates in the work of both Eastern and Western artists. There has been a discreet response by Chinese authorities to reducing the display of his portrait in public. Yet the cult of Mao continues in spite of the trauma and deaths that occurred within families, villages and provinces as a result of his leadership.

In Western literature, many comparisons have been drawn between Hitler and Mao, pondering the impact of their command. In 1994 in *The Washington Post*, Daniel Southerland detailed the investigations by the Chinese Academy of Social Sciences supported by additional academic resources that addressed the impact of the famine caused by Mao's 'Great Leap Forward', the social and economic campaign of 1948–52.[1] His major two-part article presented deeply disturbing tales of commune residents resorting to killing children or digging up the recently deceased to eat them in order to survive. And with the help of Chinese and Western scholars, Southerland was able to bring together the data to ascertain that Mao was responsible for between 50 and 80 million deaths when the statistics from the Great Leap Forward are combined with the impact of the Cultural Revolution. This research data has continued to be confirmed and supported, most recently by Yang Jisheng in his 2013 book *Tombstone*.

Hitler, by contrast, is estimated to be directly responsible for the deaths of 12 million in concentration camps and a further 30 million during World War II. According to Southerland, the numbers for Stalin are fairly similar.

Of course, neither Mao nor Hitler were observed enacting the death of anyone directly: they dictated orders. And when the impact of those orders became known – in the case of Hitler, the millions of Jews dying in camps, and in the case of Mao, the millions of deaths resulting from the Great Leap Forward and the Cultural

Revolution – they distanced themselves far enough from the atrocities but not too far from the people. During the famine, Mao gave up eating meat for six months to send a message to his people that he understood the hardship they were enduring. But he countered this apparent compassion when he also famously said:

> When there is not enough to eat, people starve to death. It is better
> to let half of the people die so that the other half can eat their fill.[2]

Strangely, the impact of Mao's revolutionary strategies, of the deaths of millions of people through force, torture or the horrific degradation of quality of life, has had very little impact on the West's approach to the image of Mao. The complacent public display of his image, indeed at times the playful interpretation and literary discussion of his image, rarely acknowledges his atrocities. It's a vastly different approach to images of Hitler, the public display of which remains carefully controlled. Any artists working with Hitler's portrait are considered to be courting controversy, and any contemporary work is immediately linked to the atrocities and legacy of the Nazi regime.

Western media has been interested in Mao since he came to power in 1949. In February of that year, *Time* magazine featured a portrait of Mao on the cover to coincide with his 'adding China to the domain of world Communism'. The momentous political declaration was, according to *Time*, a redrawing of the map of the world 'with an iron pen dipped in blood'. On the cover, Mao gazes upwards, confident in his plans for China. Just seven months later, on 1 October 1949, the People's Republic of China was founded.

Mao acted quickly on his promise of land reform, removing landholders from their farms and publicly executing and incarcerating many. Historians place the number of these class-based executions at five million, and a further six million landlords were interned in labour camps – the dreaded *laogai*. It's estimated that a total of fifty million Chinese people were subjected to the atrocities of the *laogai*, eating rotting vegetables and rats, forced into the lowest standards of living and executed in response to charges of speaking out against Communism. Others were forced into poverty, and many died of starvation due to famine.

In 1958, Mao commenced the Great Leap Forward – the policy of agricultural collectivisation that resulted in the deaths of tens of millions from famine, as well as through violence towards dissidents.

Mao entered political limbo following the failure of the Great Leap Forward; he returned to power with the Cultural Revolution. The Cultural Revolution was a 1966 Mao-endorsed call to arms against the bourgeois leanings of the party and the people, initiated in the streets of Beijing by disillusioned students who supported Mao's concerns over the 'capitalist restoration' that was becoming evident. Students took to the streets waving placards with Mao's portrait – the classic image that's often reproduced and appropriated by contemporary artists.

(The formulaic structure of the images, everyone marching in uniform and holding up their official portrait in unison, inspired American artist Annette Lemieux many years later. She copied the image for her 1991 work *Black Mass*,[3] blackening all of the portraits of Mao to suggest the utter blindness of those who follow causes without question.)

Mao's portrait also appeared in the frontispiece of his book *Quotations from Chairman Mao Tse-tung* – commonly referred to as the 'Little Red Book'. During the ten years of the Cultural Revolution, over a billion copies were printed; China's population was 735 million in 1966, and many people bought multiple copies, taking Mao's words as their personal mantra. Possession of it could save your life when you were searched by the authorities. The book was translated and distributed worldwide and continues to be sold.

Mao's teachings generated an energy among the students that flowed into zealous, violent behaviour, culminating in the deaths of millions of Chinese counter-revolutionaries, intellectuals and those considered 'elites'. The Red Guards, as the students were called, often committed spontaneous crimes against fellow Chinese citizens; their considerable wrath was particularly feared in the provinces. They were under orders from Mao and believed that their purpose was to restore a China that was united, equal and could provide a worthy future for its citizens.

The Cultural Revolution was a complex entity, with a hierarchy of players and diverse ideological and policy positions, but Mao's leadership provided guidance. And his portrait proliferated, becoming the Revolution's prevailing symbol, in spite of the Communist ideology of collective government over individualism.

It's estimated that during this time in China there were an astonishing three portraits of Mao for every person. Historian Hong Yung Lee records that it was 'dictated that every public building should put up Mao's portrait and writings; that all libraries should discard any books that contravened Mao's Thought'.[4] Mao portraits were also placed prominently within the home, strategically on the family altar – until the altars were destroyed as part of the Cultural Revolution – and if no altar existed, then it had to be hung in the main room:

> The portrait had to be treated with special care, as if it contained a divinity: nothing could be placed above it.[5]

Destruction of Mao's portrait resulted in death. It was a sign that the perpetrator did not support the ruler, and the punishment was readily and publicly enacted.

This was the fate of Zhang Hongbing's mother in 1970. Zhang, a member of the Red Guards, was only fifteen when he literally pointed the finger at his mother and denounced her to the authorities.[6] Both of his parents had been subjected to what were referred to as 'struggle' or 'criticism' sessions due to the positions of authority they held. Accounts vary as to the ferocity of the questioning during these sessions, but after two years of torment, Zhang's mother broke down. The situation in her home escalated, and her husband and son accused her of threatening to tear down Mao's portraits and contacted the authorities. Feeling isolated and under siege, she locked herself in a room and burnt a portrait of Mao.

She was taken away and killed by firing squad. Like millions of others, she was a victim of Mao's purging of elites, both intellectual and those in positions of authority, and his attempt to restore the ideal of a Communist revolution.

The Cultural Revolution's legacy continues to the present day. Contemporary Chinese artist Zhang Hongtu cuts up portraits of Mao and often places them onto Western sacred images to critique the replacing of the family altar with images of Mao. He comments:

> If one has never lived under a Communist government, Mao's portrait means nothing: it's just a popular image such as Warhol did, like Marilyn Monroe. But the first time I cut Mao's portrait with a knife and put it back together to make a new Mao image I felt guilty, sinful.[7]

In Zhang Hongtu's *Last Banquet*, thirteen Mao portraits are placed onto the faces of Jesus and the apostles. The controversial work, originally made for the 1989 exhibition *China: June 4 1989* organised by the Asian American Arts Centre in response to the Tiananmen Square protests, was later banned from a 1990 exhibition at Washington's Capitol Hill due to concerns it might offend conservative critics. Zhang was naturally bemused that a work which critiqued Chinese rule had been censored in America.[8]

The Cultural Revolution resulted in a civil war aimed at destroying the enemies of Mao's agenda. But the overwhelming viciousness and depravity of the violence forced Mao to re-evaluate his policies, and in 1971 he drew a halt to the bloodshed, enlisting the army to control China's youth.

In response, and to further the US' interest in political and economic allegiances, Mao received a visit from President Richard Nixon in February 1972. The visit was described by former US diplomat Winston Lord as a 'geopolitical earthquake': the first official contact between the West and China in over twenty years.

The meeting of the two great powers provided the West with a window into the heavily guarded, anti-Western Chinese society and their political leaders, most importantly Mao. An extraordinary media contingent accompanied the enigmatic president, who played the propaganda game himself and ensured there was plenty of material for the evening news bulletins. The cover of the 3 March 1972 issue of *Life* magazine proclaimed, 'Nixon in the Land of Mao', and the featured articles show Mao and President Nixon sitting next to each other in Mao's study; the President and his wife at official dinners; Nixon moving from table to table offering a toast to the Chinese dignitaries. The commentary muses on Nixon's intentions and the unusual lack of information imparted to the reporters – it was a show to be played on the surface, for the pictures to tell the simple story of two countries working together.[9]

It's often argued that the visit of Richard Nixon to China gave iconic Pop artist Andy Warhol free rein to do as he pleased with the portrait of Mao – that Nixon had effectively decided, for economic and political reasons, that the atrocities of the past were to be forgotten and the world was to move forward. Would that be the case if Hitler were alive and in power? It's a difficult question.

It would seem that Nixon quickly embraced the association with the power of Mao and his regime, and Warhol followed without due consideration of Mao's heritage. But a political visit does not in itself, of course, condone the visited leader's actions and views. Many dignitaries and political leaders met with Hitler prior to and during the war years – British royalty included. Famously, the Duke and Duchess of Windsor met with Hitler and collaborated with those who supported his views, their visits continuing to be the subject of political analysis. Until the Royal archives of the Duke's letters are made available, we will not know exactly the nature of the relationship; nevertheless, it is not used to justify displays of Hitler's portrait or its appropriation by artists.

Apparently, Andy Warhol read in *Life* magazine that Chairman Mao was the most famous person in the world. It would not have been the opportunity to sell to the Chinese market that attracted him, of course. Imaging of Mao in China was and still is strictly controlled, and only official portrait painters are permitted to render the image of Mao from approved photographs. Any and all other images are effectively banned.

There's nothing surprising, however, in Warhol choosing to paint a series of portraits of Mao Zedong. His attraction to the famous, the beautiful and the wealthy supported his constructed iconography and is demonstrated in his extensive series of portraits. His use of red, gold and black in many of his images of Marilyn Monroe, for example, re-imagines her as a reliquary. The *Gold Marilyn Monroe* (1962; MoMA, New York), painted in the year of her death, appears like a jewel among sixties contemporary art, which is more usually marked by angst, a commitment to abstraction or political protest. Warhol's work reflects the adoration of the Western world for its tragic icon. It is similar to the attraction he harboured for Mao – an attraction that continues to resonate in the auction houses and private and public gallery collections.

Warhol was struck by what he learnt of Mao – a man who 'suppress[ed] all other imagery and present[ed] his own visage as the dominant image in China'.[10] His view of Mao and China is particularly evident in the following statement he made to close friend David Bourdon:

> I've been reading so much about China. They're so nutty. They don't believe in creativity. The only picture they ever have is of Mao Zedong. It's great. It looks like a silkscreen.[11]

Once he'd decided upon Mao as his subject, Warhol wasted no time. Pop art is time-critical, and he needed to ensure he made the most of the congenial sentiments towards China following Nixon's 1972 visit. As his starting point, Warhol took the portrait of Mao that was reproduced inside the cover of the first edition of the Little Red Book. He initially intended to simply replicate the image through enlargement, but impressed with the impact of the portrait, he took the work further and experimented with painting over it.

Until 1972, Warhol's art practice had been largely film-making and factory-made screen-printed images, but his European dealer, Bruno Bischofberger, had encouraged him to return to painting. He executed his Mao portraits with his own hand (rather than using his studio assistants), streaking Mao's face with his typical colour permutations, enlarging the canvases to match the Communist style and emblazoning the pictures with bold reds, yellows, iridescent blues and greens. Warhol moulded and manipulated the image of Mao, providing a series of 'personalities' with the changing colours.

For the auction of one of the Mao works in London in 2011, a writer for famed auction house Christie's considered that Warhol created a 'tame bourgeois fashion motif' with his rendering of the 'pop idol' that was Mao.[12] This is the traditional position on the work – that the portraits are superficial, are fashionable entities that deliberately lack substance as portraits. The interaction of artist and sitter is considered irrelevant for these works.

There is no discussion in the Christie's auction essay of Mao's suppression of freedom of speech, or of the millions of deaths that occurred with the Cultural Revolution, as there would be if the image were of Hitler. According to a Christie's writer, the sweep of 'Communist Red' on some of the pictures 'decontaminates an image that had become a symbol of fear, rendering it inoffensive by highlighting its ubiquitous nature'.[13]

Writers and curators have often supported the view that Warhol has been able to erase the historical memory associated with Mao via his mechanisms of appropriation and energetic brushstrokes. In preparation for a sale in March 2017 at Sotheby's Hong Kong, the catalogue contains references to Warhol's *Mao* (1973; private collection) as being 'enveloped by rays of a holy and enlightened halo'. The particular portrait has conspicuous iridescent gold overpainted on and around the face. Warhol has apparently 'give[n] Mao a friendly face in the eyes of Americans'. Again, there is no discussion of the carriage of meaning for Chinese people.

In 2016, in preparation for the sale of *20 Pink Maos* (1979) by the Phillips auction house, the image was discussed as a 'quiet homage to the original source'.[14] The original source is both the image of Mao and the 1972 works produced by Warhol – the *20 Pink Maos* are reversed versions of the 1972 portraits. By the time of the production of the reversal portraits, Mao had passed away and so the schematic of the work alludes to his death through its appearance as a photographic negative. To consider the works a homage by Warhol raises some issues in relation to their source. In 1979, Warhol had not yet visited China: the portraits are only a comment on the mediated image, on the propaganda associated with Mao. The display and sale of the work is, of itself, a lack of acknowledgement of the impact of the portrait.

Part of the significance of a portrait lies in its memory associations. When we view Warhol's images of Jackie Kennedy at her husband's funeral, for example, those of us old enough to do so are immediately drawn to consider where we were on the day he died. We remember how we felt, sitting in front of a television set watching as the wind softly blew her black veil as though in slow motion, in tandem to her sense of reality at the swiftness of the events. Tears touched cheeks; Camelot was gone. The portraits locate our visual memories and connect us to this part of Western history.

Equally, the portraits of Mao connect people to his leadership, his identity and past. For some Chinese people, his face would have a similar impact as Hitler's does for those persecuted during his rule. The Cultural Revolution had begun only six years before Warhol started producing his Mao portraits, making the trauma very recent history. And Mao's atrocities were not unknown in the West; many Chinese citizens had sought political asylum in Western countries. Warhol's casual appropriation of the Mao photograph deviates from the societal rigour one would expect in relation to concern over the appropriation of the history and culture of another race without any measure of responsibility.

The first time Warhol's portraits of Mao were presented to the public was in late 1972. The *Warhol Maos* exhibition was held from 21 October to 19 November at the Kunstmuseum in Basel, Switzerland, under the stewardship of Bischofberger's gallery in Zurich. A number of paintings were purchased directly from this exhibition and have since reached as much as US$47.5 million each at auction.

Yet there appears to have been no contemporary critique of the sensitivity of the display of the portraits, either in Switzerland or elsewhere. Switzerland was the neutral site of World War II, the place where artists such as Paul Klee and Oskar Kokoschka sought refuge. Their careers in Germany were effectively obliterated when 130 and 630 of their works, respectively, were removed from German museums before the war, an indication that their work was not supported by the Nazi regime.

Kokoschka, along with many other refugees, was still alive and living in Switzerland when the Warhol portraits of Mao were exhibited. The impact of World War II remained very clear in 1972, and it is unlikely that the exhibition of portraits of another dictator would have rested easily.

In 1974, the exhibition *Andy Warhol: Mao* was held at the Musée Galliera (now the Palais Galliera) in Paris, as part of its *Painters Bearing Witness to Their Time* series – on a wall covered with Warhol's Mao wallpaper. It's doubtful that the refined enclave of the Musée would have exhibited portraits of Hitler in this way. Thirty years after Paris was liberated from Nazi Germany, the memory was still fresh. Indeed, the Musée is located on the Avenue Pierre 1er de Serbie, less than ten minutes from the former Gestapo headquarters of World War II. The headquarters were renovated post-war, but in a few deliberately preserved cells it's possible to read the scrawled notes of those about to be killed, tortured or sent to a concentration camp. Yet the gallery welcomed Warhol's *Maos*.

It's surprising how few have expressed concern at Warhol's images of Mao, given the level of antagonism to portraiture of other leaders responsible for death on such a massive scale. The actor Dennis Hopper did once shoot at a work he owned, but only because he was spooked by the Chairman staring at him when he returned home late one night! The deep-blue *Mao* still has the two bullet holes

Figure 15 Alessandro Allori (1535–1607), *Portrait of Grand Duchess Bianca Cappello de Medici with Her Son*, c.1580–1614, oil on canvas, 128.42 × 100.48 cm. The Karl and Esther Hoblitzelle Collection, gift of the Hoblitzelle Foundation. Image: Dallas Museum of Art

Figure 16 *Portrait of Catherine of Aragon*, English School (16th century), oil on panel, 52 × 42 cm. Lambeth Palace, London. Image: Bridgeman Images

Figure 17 Jacopo Primavera (active c.1575–1588), *Mary Stuart, Queen of Scots, 1542–1587*, lead. Samuel H. Kress Collection. Image: National Gallery of Art, Washington, DC

Figure 18 Mao Zedong portrait on Gate of Heavenly Peace, Tiananmen Square, Beijing, 2012, photograph, 41.4 × 31.6 cm. Image: Gavin Hellier/Alamy Stock Photo

Figure 19 Workers remove the second of four statues of Confederate heroes at the University of Texas in a surprise midnight action before fall classes began in late August, 21 August 2017, photograph, 25 × 25.1 cm. Image: Bob Daemmrich/ Alamy Stock Photo

Figure 20 Ground floor, Wasserstein Hall, Harvard University, 25 October 2017, photograph. Image: Julie Cotter

Portraits of Harvard Law School professors hang on the wall.

Figure 21 *Captain Cook Statue Vandalised*, 25 January 2018, photograph, 35.3 × 24.2 cm.
Image: Nicole Garmston

Figure 22 Tom Roberts (1856–1931), *Dick Rotumah*, 1892, pen and ink on paper,
17.2 × 35.6 cm. Image: State Library of New South Wales, Sydney

Figure 23 Etienne Cohen and Paul Davis, Bondi Indigenous mural, 2013,
painting on side of Wayside Chapel (destroyed). Image: Steven Salgo

Figure 24 John Everett Millais (1829–1896), *Thomas Carlyle*, 1877, oil on canvas, 116.8 × 88.3 cm. Image: National Portrait Gallery, London

The gashes inflicted by Anne Hunt across Carlyle's face are still visible on the portrait.

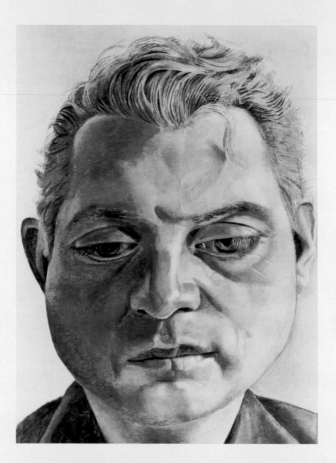

Figure 25 Lucian Freud (1922–2011), *Wanted*, 2001, colour litho.
Image: Private collection/© The Lucian Freud Archive/Bridgeman Images

through the canvas: one that pierced clear through his eyelid, and the other to the left side of his cheek.[15]

The treatment of a body of work by German-born artist Anselm Kiefer provides an interesting contrast. In 1969, he undertook a series in which he was photographed dressed in his father's military uniform and standing by a number of European monuments while giving the *Sieg heil*. These works were generally considered to be in poor taste. They were undertaken only three years before Warhol's series of Mao portraits.

Kiefer has subsequently produced a considerable body of work referencing the killing fields, the ruins and the desolation of war – and continues to be chastised for reminding Germany and the rest of the world of its horrors and their perpetrators. The works are usually discussed within the context of the Jewish genocide and the death toll of Hitler's rule, with his focus upon German suffering and German people causing concern. The general view is that, as writer Charles Darwent put it, Kiefer's 'failure to bury the past made him complicit in it'.[16]

Kiefer has also worked with the image of Mao. His 2000 work *Let a Thousand Flowers Bloom*, now in New York's Metropolitan Museum of Art, presents the Communist leader as a faded figure standing in salute, Kiefer adding paint, sand, ash and charcoal to torn photographs as a sign of the passage of time. The image of Mao references Kiefer's positioning of himself as Hitler. Through the work, he deliberately asks the viewer to consider the similarities that exist between the two leaders.

Western society has assisted China in erasing the horrors of Mao's rule. While officially China does not agree with Warhol's approach to portraiture and what could be deemed a defacing of Mao's portrait, there must also be a quiet satisfaction by the ruling party about the support it provides to China and its statesmen. The portraits assist the Chinese policy of maintaining Mao's image as a historical figure, reinforcing the erasure of the records of the millions of deaths caused by Mao and defining the Chinese leadership as a secure body capable of guiding over a billion people. The Mao portrait is an important Chinese asset.

A Communist Party communiqué issued in 1981 relates to the hanging of portraits of leaders in China, particularly those of Mao, and reminds the public that moderation must be exercised and excessive numbers of portraits should not be hung, so as not to offend 'international sensibilities'. A line-up of Mao portraits on Mao wallpaper is, of course, far beyond the Chinese 'homage'.

Indeed, China's refusal to display Warhol's Mao portraits confounds the West: the Chinese people are considered to be incapable of countenancing an alternative view – of opening up to the creative response of Western society. The 2013 exhibition of Warhol's work that toured a number of Chinese cities, *Andy Warhol: 15 Minutes Eternal*, did not include the Mao portraits that were originally selected for the exhibition. When Warhol's *Mao* (1973) was included in the Sotheby's 2017 Hong Kong auction, there was significant media interest and a suggestion that China was relaxing its opposition to Warhol's appropriation of the portrait. The symbolic embrace was applauded. Alternatively, Western support remains for Germany's ban on all imagery of Hitler. There is a complexity in the views and laws of both governments. There are, of course, people in Germany who believe the image of Hitler should still be displayed, either to remind the populace of his atrocities or simply because they followed his beliefs and their parents fought for him.

The official contemporary Chinese position on the period of rule by Mao Zedong is to express criticism of his policies after 1958. After his death, he was famously declared to have been 70 per cent right and 30 per cent wrong, and during the course of the 11th Central Committee of the Communist Party of China, from 1977 to 1982, it was resolved to completely denounce the Cultural Revolution.

In 1980, the Communist Party issued a communiqué regarding the removal of Mao statues. In accordance with the policy of 'cutting back on propagating individuals', it stated that statues could gradually be reduced – but not all taken down at once. There was concern that any abrupt activity could garner controversy and debate, as had occurred with the removal of a statue of Mao at Mengjin, located in Henan Province. The statue was demolished without consultation, resulting in public controversy and prompting the 1980 communiqué. It was actually usual for Mao statues to be removed without notice; what was unusual was the public response. In May 1988, esteemed writer W.J.T. Mitchell took a photo of a more than nine-metre-tall

bamboo-covered statue of Mao while visiting Beijing University –
the next day, to his surprise, it had been reduced to rubble.[17]

In 2016, an extraordinary golden statue was erected in Tongxu,
also situated in Henan Province. It rose more than thirty-six metres
above quiet, undulating pastures, until it was unceremoniously
removed by authorities during the final stages of construction. Images
of the enormous, gleaming structure had reached international social
media, to much ridicule, and it was immediately destroyed. It didn't
go unnoticed by the media that the statue was being constructed in
the province that suffered the most deaths from the famine resulting
from the Great Leap Forward.

Nonetheless, the image of Mao Zedong remains a prominent
symbol in China. Mao's political history and influence naturally
directs much of that symbolism, but the longevity of his image can
also be traced to sources in popular culture. When visiting Beijing,
for example, it is impossible to miss the immense portrait of Mao that
continues to be displayed in Tiananmen Square [Figure 18]. A 1982
photograph by Christopher Makos taken of Warhol during his first
and only visit to China has him standing in front of the Tiananmen
Square portrait awkwardly fidgeting, brow furrowed. Mao's portrait
is intrinsic to the record of the tourist experience in China.

Mao's portrait was first displayed in Tiananmen Square in 1949 –
replacing the portrait of previous leader Chiang Kai-shek, which in
turn replaced the portrait of Sun Yat-sen, the founder of the Chinese

Republic. More than forty years after Mao's death, his 6 × 4.6-metre oil portrait continues to dominate the 40-hectare square. There were reportedly up to eight versions during his lifetime, allowing the portrait to 'age' with him. The side view of Mao that was made popular during the Cultural Revolution was later replaced by the current frontal view showing both his ears, an image that signified he was listening to all.

The portrait deteriorates rapidly due to environmental effects, so each year on Chinese National Day, 1 October, official artist Ge Xiaoguang ceremonially presents a newly painted copy. The old portrait is removed, covered over in white paint and placed in a guarded vault along with the other 'white' paintings, to prevent them ever resurfacing.

It's easy to be seduced by the 'popularity' of the Tiananmen Square portrait. Tourists flock to it, while armed guards ensure order and protection. It could be argued that public response to the portrait is contained, sedate – a contrast to the response that would be anticipated to a display of Hitler's portrait. While political activists and artists such as Ai Weiwei challenge the symbols of the Chinese ruling party, Chinese people, in general, regard Mao's portrait with both ambivalence and respect. For some, the portrait in Tiananmen Square is nothing more than the fashionable icon that attracted Warhol and is a drawcard for tourists, while others gaze upon his face and remember the hardship and atrocities of his rule. A few Chinese people, despite their government's efforts to present Mao as largely benevolent, have targeted the portrait as a symbol of repression.

In 1989, three young men alighted from a packed train as it pulled into Beijing and headed to Tiananmen Square. They'd felt compelled to journey to the capital from their small town in Hunan Province (the early home of Mao), their passage largely funded by supporters, to join the thousands of students in the square protesting for 'freedom, democracy and human rights'. However, in spite of the enormous group in attendance and their energy for the protest, the three young men felt ineffectual, that they were on the outer. The protest was not proceeding as they had envisaged.

One of the men, Yu Zhijian, gave an interview to *China Change* in June 2005, explaining their collective disillusionment and the options they discussed for protest. One was self-immolation, and the other was to 'take action against Mao Zedong's portrait . . . [and] put a symbolic end to the repressive Communist regime'.[18] They chose the latter option and set about planning to physically take down the portrait. However, its size prevented the three lithe men from taking such an action alone and, to their chagrin, they had no support from fellow protesters, who felt they were too reactionary. In light of the numerous obstacles, they momentously decided to change plans. They filled two dozen or so eggshells with paint, unfurled a banner for liberty, and proceeded to hurl the eggs with all their might at the portrait of Mao.

While it is unlikely that the three men had any knowledge of Warhol's Mao portraits, their splattering of the portrait is reminiscent of Warhol's graffiti-style approach to his Mao paintings, the slash of red paint across the chest of the 4.5-metre version in the Art Institute of Chicago quite typical.

The action of the young men made news headlines around the world. The paint-splattered portrait was swiftly covered with a brown tarpaulin by authorities; the student body handed the 'Hunan rebels', Yu Zhijian and his companions Yu Dongyue and Lu Decheng, over to the authorities with similar alacrity.

There was a secret trial in the basement of the Beijing Intermediate People's Court, at which the three men were provided with an opportunity to make a statement, although they knew it would be of no benefit. Yu Dongyue proclaimed that the work was performance art, not political. Lu's wife, Wang Quiping, pleaded with the judge for her husband's life to be spared, asking, 'Are you people going to sentence these three to death for a mere picture?'[19] For his 'grave crime', Yu Dongyue was sentenced to twenty years in jail, of which he served nearly seventeen. Yu Zhijian was sentenced to life in prison but released after eleven years; Lu was given sixteen years and released after almost nine.

Their true objective, of course, had been to fight for the abolition of the Communist regime: destroy the symbol and they might have a chance. Indeed, it was the protection of the symbol of Mao that was the focus of one of the prosecutors sent to interrogate Lu. He considered the attack on the portrait to be personal and indicative of Lu's past reactionary behaviour. 'You have no love for Chairman Mao!' he stated. 'You did not cry for Chairman Mao at his memorial.'[20] Clearly the prosecutor's emotional connection to Mao guided his interrogation. Like many of the protestors in Tiananmen Square, he believed in Mao's divinity, that the Chairman was untouchable no matter one's political beliefs.

As Geremie Barmé has explored, there was a rise in the cult of Mao in China in the 1980s, largely due to political uncertainty and a lack of confidence in the future. He comments that many Chinese people 'could indulge in Mao nostalgia because due to bans on remembering the past they had forgotten its horrors'.[21] While the Hunan rebels had fought in defiance of past atrocities, remembered and discussed within their enclave, the protesters in Beijing had left the past behind in anticipation of a better future, hoping for greater individual freedom. Yet the Tiananmen Square protests, and perhaps also the actions of the Hunan rebels who committed one of the most hated crimes in China – the splattering of Mao's portrait in Tiananmen with paint – actually increased the popularity of Mao's portrait in China. According to Barmé's research, in 1989 only 370,000 copies of the portrait of Mao had been sold; in 1990 this increased dramatically to 22.95 million, and in 1991 it was 50 million.

The response of the West to the attack on the portrait was revealing. *The New York Times* reported the event on 24 May 1989, quoting the support from the crowd for Mao, while other news agencies reported on the handing over of the Hunan rebels by the student group. Interestingly, at the Museum of Modern Art (MoMA) in New York, a Warhol retrospective had recently concluded, at which gallery visitors had stood quietly in front of his paint-splattered images of Mao. The world had begun to take note of the hundreds of thousands of protesters assembling in Tiananmen Square in mid-April, the MoMA exhibition continuing until 2 May.

Of course, the Tiananmen protests culminated in the 4 June massacre and incarceration of protesters, with many of those arrested never seen again. There were Western sanctions on China and outrage; Australia granted permanent visas to 42,000 students and their families, while other countries including the US reached out with similar aid. Yet research by George Washington University has revealed that, to maintain relations with China, the US government conveyed a secret message to the authorities indicating that they viewed the events of Tiananmen Square as an 'internal affair'.[22]

The Warhol portraits of Mao remain untarnished by the massacre. It was left to the writer Don DeLillo, in his fictional work *Mao II*, to consider the impact of cultural producers upon the individual and the manner in which Warhol is able to distance Mao from his actions. He writes a dark tale of American life, Warhol's *Mao* series symbolic of the hierarchy of the image over everything.[23] And perhaps that is the key to Warhol's portraits of Mao: that he knew the Western world would not be able to resist them, that a choice would be made to gloss over Mao's history in favour of the portrait.

Warhol's portraits of Mao are considered a commentary on the mediated image, on the propaganda associated with Mao. At times, they mock the image of Mao with the slashings of paint that cover his body and the makeup-like appearance that gives him the persona of a performance artist. There is no acknowledgement that for many the portrait conjures the death of loved ones, the incarceration and exile of family, and the hopelessness of lost dreams.

Attacks on the portrait in Tiananmen Square continue sporadically. In April 2015 a Chinese man, Sun Bing, was sentenced to fourteen months in prison for throwing a bottle of ink at the portrait of Mao, smearing black marks across the lower corner. The ink made only a small impression on the portrait and was quickly cleaned away. His actions highlight the conflict of Mao and the layering of meaning within the portrait. Warhol's appropriation of the portrait creates a further layer that encapsulates a Western view.

Over the years, Western society has had access to a consistent and solid narrative of the atrocities committed under Mao's rule, but support for Warhol's portraits has never faltered. They are now too valuable to destroy – too valuable to meet the same fate as Gerhard Richter's painting of Hitler. As discussed, they are generally considered within an art-historical framework rather than deliberated upon in the context of attributable deaths.

In 2015, when Warhol's *Mao* (1972) sold for an astonishing US$47.5 million, the catalogue writer described the Mao portraits as reducing 'an irreproachable image power to the level of surface decoration'.[24] The writer considers Warhol to be subverting Mao's power and control.

It's an approach that has a significant lineage – Diego Velázquez's 1650 *Portrait of Pope Innocent X* (Galleria Doria Pamphilj, Rome) is one such example. Considered by many to be the greatest portrait ever executed, Velázquez's unflattering portrayal casts the Pope cloaked in an aura of mistrust. Pope Innocent X had deliberately sought and initiated conflict and violent resolutions throughout his reign. He had many to fear. Velázquez sought to convey that anxiety rather than explore an image of power. It is extraordinary that papal approval was bestowed upon the portrait in spite of the obvious subversion of power.

Yet unlike Warhol, Velázquez was embedded in the society in which he worked. There's a reason that Velázquez is one of the greatest portrait painters. He sat with his subjects in studios, palaces and cathedrals to capture their likeness. He interacted with them, understood the way they might part their lips at an odd thought, rest their hand limply upon an armrest rather than hold it with strength and purpose. He mingled with the people who advised, lived with, or served those subjects, and cast an exceedingly intelligent eye over the society. Warhol, by contrast, casually appropriated the Mao photograph and with it, the history and culture of Chinese people.

A Christie's writer described one of Warhol's Mao portraits as 'present[ing] its famous sober-faced icon as if lost or dissolving into a glamorised swathe of synthetic colour'.[25] The luscious exteriors of the paintings sanction writers, gallery staff and collectors to gloss over the mass killings of Mao's regime; indeed, the works help to legitimise the parade of his image.

In 1980, Warhol's *Ten Portraits of Jews of the Twentieth Century* was exhibited at the Jewish Museum in New York, the link between the subject matter of the work and the museum obvious. The works can be considered within his interest in mortality given that all of the subjects were deceased, an interest some critics at the time found macabre and disingenuous. The subjects include Sigmund Freud, the Marx Brothers and Albert Einstein. The *New York Times* critic Hilton Kramer considered the way the exhibition exploited the 'Jewish subjects without showing the slightest grasp of their significance is offensive – or would be, anyway, if the artist had not already treated so many non-Jewish subjects in the same tawdry manner'.[26] It is of interest that such an opinion of Warhol's glib treatment of his subjects has not been obviously extended to the Mao portraits. A restaging of the Jewish exhibition some thirty years later in museums around the world inspired a more considered debate that had as its focus the nature of the Jewish contribution to arts and sciences.

Importantly, one of the few times that the Warhol imaging of Mao has been critiqued was when placed beside the work of Chinese artist and political activist Ai Weiwei in the 2016 *Andy Warhol | Ai Weiwei* exhibition in Australia. Dissident political expression is fundamental to the work of Ai, the son of a Chinese poet forced into a labour camp under Mao's rule – he was considered one of the intellectual elites. In 2011, Ai was incarcerated for eighty-one days without charge by the Chinese government. There was an outcry around the world, protests occurring across America and the European Union, and lengthy petitions demanding his release. The Chinese government claimed there were instances of tax evasion that eventually led to his wife being charged and fined.

Ai's work provides a context for the many political prisoners in China, just as the portrait images included in the installations by French artist Christian Boltanski remind us of the Jewish people who lost their lives at the hands of Hitler. Ai has spread 100 million porcelain sunflower seeds on gallery floors as a means to represent the downtrodden Chinese people. Communist propaganda placed Mao as the sun and the people as the sunflowers. Ai has painted portraits of a laughing Mao as a reference to the life he lived under state power – Mao ever the leader distinct and separate from the momentous suffering of his people.

Perhaps, as John Curley suggests in a catalogue essay accompanying the *Andy Warhol | Ai Weiwei* exhibition:

> [The] *Mao* portraits should be conceived in opposition to the figure of the Chairman; the freedom of Warhol's painterly expression demonstrates the constructed mythology of the oppressive dictator.[27]

It is not a common position to raise the notion of Mao as oppressive dictator in relation to Warhol's portraits. Curley suggests that Warhol is taking a stand against Mao, that he is actively situating the gloss and mythology of Mao in such a way that society will seek what lies beneath – the mind of the dictator behind the painted face. He is placing the historical actions of the subject firmly at the centre of the portrait rather than the mediated view of a pop culture product.

There are some writers who do question the context of Warhol's Mao portraits. In a discussion of the opening of a Warhol exhibition in Los Angeles in 2002, Jennifer Doyle noted that the mayor, curator and director gave their speeches in front of a Mao portrait. She commented that the 'Mao can never be fully emptied out of its historical force', and pondered how the opening would have been accommodated if there had been an Asian audience. Fittingly, she remarks that we are meant to view Warhol as an 'existential exercise in nothingness'.[28]

Contemporary Chinese artist Yu Youhan appropriates the traditional image of Mao – a risky enterprise even in today's China – overlaying the image with stylised parodies of Western art, Warhol's works among them. Yu critiques the cult of Mao in China and the superficial intrigue of the West with the image of Mao, exploring the role the image has played in Yu's own life. His use of the image of Mao indirectly references the student protests in Tiananmen Square; he plays with the image, a sign that Chinese society is relaxing attitudes to artistic freedom following 1989.

Warhol's *Maos* remain as familiar and popular as ever. Mao-portrait dinner plates are sold in the MoMA Design Store, posters of the portraits are plastered up in student accommodation, and the astronomically priced original paintings adorn some of the most respected galleries and wealthiest homes in the world.

The artist Louise Lawler photographs artworks displayed in galleries or on the walls of auction houses, asking the viewer to consider the owner of the work as intrinsic to its meaning. There's considerable social status, for example, in the ownership of a Warhol painting. Lawler subtly turns Warhol's commodity-building on its head and re-photographs his work – auction label and all, her work *Does Andy Warhol Make You Cry?* (1988) includes Warhol's 1962 painting *Round Marilyn* at auction. Her secondary image appropriation places a further barrier between the original work and the viewer. It reminds us that it is simply a commodity, and we are merely a part of the process. There is nothing to be gained from looking too closely. She succinctly maps Warhol's pessimistic view of American life.

Yet it is the statement by Chinese American author Anchee Min that provides the context for the Mao portrait in contemporary Chinese society. In her memoir, she recalls her surprise when she commenced her art studies in America:

> I couldn't understand why Mao portraits were up in American museums and our classroom when a billion Chinese tried to take them down. We finally took the Mao buttons off our jackets, the Mao portraits off our walls, and Mao's quotations out of our conversations. I asked the professor 'Why Mao?' He shrugged and said 'I don't know.'[29]

CHAPTER 6

Whitewash:
Erasing Black History
in the West

In the sophisticated, conceptual, egalitarian world of contemporary art, it is rare to encounter a request for a portrait to be destroyed. It just doesn't seem to fit the spirit of freedom of expression that is intrinsic to the profession of curators, artists, academics, writers and the viewing public – particularly when the work is displayed in the context of a gallery space in a biennale with an international reputation. Galleries are generally designated as safe refuges where politics, sexuality, race or perhaps the notion of art practice can be challenged and explored.

When Dana Schutz's portrait of Emmett Till, *Open Casket* (private collection), was exhibited for the first time in September 2016 at the Contemporary Fine Arts Gallery in Berlin, there was literally no sound. The show was titled *Waiting for the Barbarians* (after the J. M. Coetzee novel) and consisted of mostly large, stridently coloured paintings, some whimsical while others tackled more serious matters. Subjects as random as the volatile *Fight in an Elevator* (2015) were indicative of works that speculated on the unease and disparate nature of contemporary society. The work *Open Casket* was not discussed in the press release that accompanied the exhibition, and the story of the work appears not to have been a focus. The painting received quite a different reception when exhibited in the 2017 Whitney Biennial as one of three of Schutz's paintings chosen for the prestigious event.

Chicago-born Emmett Till was savagely beaten, tortured and shot before his fourteen-year-old body was thrown in Mississippi's Tallahatchie River in 1955. He had been taken from his bed in his uncle's house and set upon by two white men who were angry that he, a young African American boy, had apparently wolf-whistled and physically assaulted the wife of one of the men. His disfigured body was pulled from the river and, in spite of the best attempts of the Sheriff to have him buried immediately, Emmett's mother, Mamie Till-Mobley, insisted on the body being returned to his home in Chicago. The request for the return of the body was conditional on the casket remaining closed. Yet Emmett's mother wanted the face of a victim of racism, torture and murder to be exposed; she said, 'let the people see what I've seen'.[1] The men were charged with murder but acquitted by an all-male, all-white jury. The men admitted to the murder the following year in a paid interview in *Look* magazine. In America, you cannot be tried twice for a crime.

Photographs of Emmett can be viewed over the internet today, his swollen, bruised face in stark contrast to the starched white shirt chosen for his funeral dress. The body was exhumed in 2005 as part of an action to have the case reopened and although unsuccessful, it highlights the continuing passion behind the desire for justice for Emmett. The casket that housed Emmett's body could not be reburied and, donated by Emmett's family, is exhibited at the Smithsonian's National Museum of African American History and Culture. The restored casket on display is a deliberate act of memory and action. The family hopes that it will act as a focus for individual inspiration, to encourage the dissemination of Emmett's story and lead those who view the casket to consider one thing: 'If I had been there in 1955 I would have done all I could to help that family'.[2] The wife of the perpetrator, many years later, retracted her story of the assault. The injustice of the system, the age of the boy and the inspirational strength of Mamie Till-Mobley helped to inspire the black rights movement that was evolving during this time.

Upon the day of the opening of the 2017 Whitney Biennial to the public, artist Hannah Black took to her Facebook page and posted a statement that questioned the authority of a white artist to once again appropriate a race narrative from black culture. For Black, the painting represented systemic oppression. Her request was not that the painting be removed from the show – she made an urgent recommendation that it be destroyed. Her concern was that a white person was able to, without regard, 'transmute Black suffering into profit and fun, though the practice has been normalized for a long time'.[3] The profit was associated with the high prices commanded by Schutz for her work, although this portrait has never been for sale. The fun is difficult to comprehend. The picture, while painted in Schutz's typically rich, expressionistic style, is not easily digested and in turn suggests the wretchedness of what happened to Emmett. Pictures of the painting on the crisp white gallery walls add a further depth of loneliness to the work itself. We don't really want to look at this painting and think about Emmett's final hours.

The debate that ensued across all media was heated. How could a privileged white female artist in the twenty-first century identify with the life of Emmett Till, or indeed, any person of African American heritage, and does she have the authority to 'use' that story? There was also opposition from the other side – outrage within the arts community that an artist had called for the destruction of a work of art. The debate extended to a planned exhibition of Schutz's work at the Institute of Contemporary Art in Boston in 2017, which was targeted with calls that it should be cancelled, despite the fact that it did not include *Open Casket*. The Boston exhibition did go ahead but with enhanced signage and educational programs.

Hannah Black was concerned about the suffering and oppression that was the story of her heritage – that the use of the image by Schutz was an offhand white appropriation of an image that signified for black people the struggle that was an intrinsic part of their lives. It is worth reflecting upon a statement that she wrote in relation to the picture:

> Although Schutz's intention may be to present white shame, this shame is not correctly represented as a painting of a dead Black boy by a white artist – those non-Black artists who sincerely wish to highlight the shameful nature of white violence should first of all

stop treating Black pain as raw material. The subject matter is not Schutz's; white free speech and white creative freedom have been founded on the constraint of others, and are not natural rights. The painting must go.[4]

The statement was co-signed by artists, curators, commentators and academics but later withdrawn from Black's Facebook page. She presents a perspective that highlights the lack of power within her community to own their stories. Yet it could be argued that Schutz humanises for a younger community that is ignorant of Emmett Till's fate the murder that occurred over sixty years ago. Schutz explained her response as one of anguish as only a mother can feel. Previously, in conversation with artist Nigel Cooke about the nature of portraiture, she commentated that a painting 'can reorder the world in a physical way. A painting can act as a person'.[5] Schutz was discussing her hypothetical 2005 picture *The Autopsy of Michael Jackson*. Painted four years before his death, the work was not subject to accusations of white power and appropriation – perhaps because of Jackson's position of wealth and authority within the community. During the 2017 Whitney Biennial, artist Parker Bright protested silently in front of *Open Casket* in a manner that felt protective, as though he was governing the spirit of Emmett Till. Upon his T-shirt he had written the words 'Black Death Spectacle'.

The ethics of the appropriation of a black story by a white artist do not disappear with the destruction of the portrait, nor does the story of Emmett Till. We have to ask if Schutz's work – which brings to the fore his suffering, known in America but not to me, an Australian writer – is justified. I cannot imagine the response of Emmett Till's family to the portrait or the outrage that has continually been felt by African American people. But to view the portrait is a choice – it requires attendance in a gallery space and the payment of an entry fee – which ensures a physical interaction with the work in the context of other works in the gallery. The dissemination of the work over the internet cannot be controlled but the work still needs to be found on this platform. The Whitney Museum naturally rejected the request to destroy the work. They asked the public to trust their ability to challenge, engage and inspire debate. Social media likened the debate that included the call for the portrait's destruction to the burning of books in World War II.

Society is reconciling and confronting the past atrocities enacted by wealthy, white (predominantly) men. The opportunity to address the power structures that led to the atrocities and to investigate the singularity of that power within contemporary ideals of acceptable behaviour has been recently triggered by public opposition to past visual memorialising.

It is difficult to imagine walking by a statue of Robert E. Lee every single day if you are a descendant of slaves owned by him and have no choice but to pass his imposing body: the magnificence of the bronze form, dew glistening on the shoulders of his uniform as you quickly walk to work on a winter's day, the outline of the sculpture looking dark and ominous in the warm, damp air of a summer evening as you head home to cook or study or dine with friends. As Marcel Proust reminds us:

> our social personality is a creation of the thoughts of other people. Even the simple act which we describe as 'seeing someone we know' is to some extent an intellectual process. We pack the physical outline of the person we see with all the notions we have already formed about him.[6]

You would not previously have been able to avoid such an encounter as you made your way across the South Mall of the University of Texas (UT); indeed, six prominent Confederate statues lined your path until they were all removed by August 2017 [Figure 19].[7] Following the Charleston church shooting in 2015, the mass shooting whereby a white supremacist massacred nine African Americans during a prayer service, students became increasingly opposed to the memorialising of Confederate leaders' achievements on their university campus. The statues occasioned an innate life of their own, reminding all that the subjects had fought for the values of the Confederacy.

Meanwhile, in 1999 a Martin Luther King Jr statue was installed in the East Mall of UT away from the Confederate group. Funded largely by students as a symbolic step to bring students together on the campus, it was initially vandalised until cameras were installed, the decision by UT to display a statue of the man who symbolised the African American civil rights movement clearly a concern for some. The statue represents the fight for equality and respect, the recent

Black Lives Matter campaign publicly highlighting the inequality of targeted violence and racial profiling by the justice system.

A visit to a memorial statue that is presented as a portrait of the subject, a statue that is designed to embody the physicality of society's nominated heroes, provides the opportunity to engage with that physicality and consider relationships to family and society. The Martin Luther King statue, for example, no doubt inspires stories of survival and prejudice and encourages debate. It is a deliberate and conscious act to erect a statue – a public statement that symbolises the attitude of contemporary society to a historical past.

In 1866, following the end of the American Civil War, Robert E. Lee took the time to write to one of his former Major Generals, Thomas L. Rosser, warning of the consequences of erecting statues.

> As regards the erection of such a monument as is contemplated; my conviction is, that however grateful it would be to the feelings of the South, the attempt in the present condition of the Country, would have the effect of retarding, instead of accelerating its accomplishment; & of continuing, if not adding to, the difficulties under which the Southern people labour.[8]

A Robert E. Lee statue was installed on the South Mall at UT in 1933 and was included in the count by the Southern Poverty Institute of 718 Confederate statues and monuments to be found across America on public property. Most of the statues were not erected until the height of what is known as the 'Jim Crow' era – the period between 1877 and the 1950s when the segregation and disenfranchisement laws that determined the way of life for African Americans were introduced. Timing is important in the re-evaluation of the statues and the debate on their removal. Lee's warning was heeded and the majority were not commissioned in the immediate post-Civil War period when the opportunity for commemoration of war leadership might have been the most appropriate. The erection of the statues in the thirties was a sign to the general public that the sentiments and beliefs of the right to fight for Confederate ideals were appropriate. The campus statues have mostly been reassigned to displays in the UT museums or to storage.

The Stone Mountain Carving in Georgia was touted as the eighth wonder of the world when it was officially 'unveiled' by Vice-President Spiro Agnew in 1970. The carving depicts three grim, stern faces of Confederates: Jefferson Davis, Robert E. Lee and Thomas 'Stonewall' Jackson. The monument, stretching across more than a hectare of rock face, was not conceived until the early twentieth century when it was commissioned by the United Daughters of the Confederacy (UDC) and carving commenced in 1923. While the UDC still exists today, and the daughters proclaim their abhorrence of racist, hateful activity, President General Patricia Bryson considers that the memorial statues, like the UDC members, 'have stayed quietly in the background, never engaging in public controversy'.[9] It was a photograph in the Minneapolis Black Forest Inn, *Generals of the Daughters of the American Revolution* (1963) by Richard Prince, that was shot at, twice, by a disgruntled patron. The photo survives with the bullet holes.

The issues of display of past leaders are not quite that simple. As the Southern Poverty Law Center has investigated, the Stone Mountain rock face was on the private land of an associate of the Ku Klux Klan, with regular meetings held at the top of the rock face.

Significant delays resulted in the abandoning of the Stone Mountain Carving until 1958, the period of the civil rights movement, when the State of Georgia decided to take on responsibility for its completion. It is the association of the history of the monument with racist activity that brings into question the motives of those behind the monument. While the stated objectives of the UDC are to memorialise their forefathers who they believe were abiding by their patriotic duty, the carved hand-on-heart of each of the figures symbolic of this, they do not accept the hurt and trauma such statues suggest to those whose families were subjugated by enslavement and white supremacist views. Bryson clearly states: 'We are saddened that some people find anything connected with the Confederacy to be offensive'. Robert E. Lee inherited slaves from his mother and oversaw the Arlington plantation slaves, his cruelty and punishment as well as the breaking-up of families through the sale of a number of slaves well documented. The testimonies of Lee ordering brine to be poured on the backs of those who had been whipped to ensure the punishment was appropriately administered are hard to forget.[10]

The stories of slave punishment challenge the espoused views of the Lost Cause of benevolence that followed the war, its meaning embedded in the apparent compassion shown towards the slaves.

Preservation of the views and standards of a community through the commemorative is often a framework to guide contemporary perspectives on past actions. President Donald Trump hangs the portrait of Andrew Jackson, the 7th President of the United States, in his office. General Jackson was a slave-owning planter who permitted his slaves to be whipped to increase productivity and, as President, signed the Indian Removal Act in 1830 as well as ordered the massacres of Native American tribes. There is a continuing call for his statues to be removed.

President Trump has commented, 'Sad to see the history and culture of our great country being ripped apart with the removal of our beautiful statues and monuments'.[11] Indeed, the heroic and impenetrable nature of a statue can provide little opportunity to engage with the vicissitudes of the actions of the past. Taking down a statue does not destroy history – it just removes the symbol from public view. The removal is a sign to families desecrated by the inhuman actions of a historical figure and to those who continue to support the underlying premises of such barbaric practices that society not only has a point of view regarding such barbarism but has enacted laws to prevent it.

The impact of past symbols upon the Harvard Law School community became a debate embedded in community beliefs following the dissemination of research in 2000 by eminent legal historian and Harvard Law School Professor Daniel Coquillette.

Professor Coquillette unearthed the background to the design of the Harvard Law School shield, authorised for use in 1937 and based on a crest used by the wealthy slave-owning Isaac Royall family. It was Isaac Royall Jr who provided the original endowment for Professor of Law to the Harvard Corporation. In response to Coquillette's revelations and the gradual awareness within the broader community of the significance of specific, racially invested symbols, protests occurred in 2015 at Harvard University. A specially convened Harvard Law School Committee later recommended removal of the shield following extensive consultation with staff and students. The growing public concern also raised issues for the Royall House and Slave Quarters museum in Medford, Massachusetts. The museum tells the story of slavery, the conditions under which slaves lived, while also placing into historical context the Royall family story.

The protests at Harvard University involved a group called Royall Must Fall, a movement of students advocating for the decolonisation of the campus, as well as those with an opposing view who considered past symbology should not be tampered with, as there were lessons to be learnt within that symbolism. The battle over public memory came to a head in November 2015 when portraits of African American law professors were found vandalised as a sign that not everyone believes in a campus of equality and respect. In October 2017, I visited the Harvard Law School in order to engage with the nature and impact of the racist attack on staff.

Wasserstein Hall, the new and spectacular building that is at the heart of the Harvard Law School, was bustling with activity as I entered and found my way along the soft-polished floors

[Figure 20]. Lectures had just finished and a flood of students emerged from wood-panelled doors to cross over to their next lecture. There were no blisteringly loud echoes that you usually find in such university halls, the conversations were subdued, no one shouted; this is a place to learn the skills that will take the students to all corners of our fraught and disturbed globe. The students here will hopefully garner the abilities to negotiate in a considered, sophisticated manner and learn to rise above the desire within some communities for violence, abuse and disregard for the rights of all. I sat in the quiet spaces of the lounge on the first floor. As I observed these environs of intense learning and debate, the act of vandalism upon the university professors' portraits appeared all the more horrific.

Professor Ronald S. Sullivan Jr, a Faculty Director at Harvard Law School, greeted me as though we were long lost friends. I waited outside his office while he finished a consultation with a student who left effusive in her praise of his assistance. That's what law professors do. They guide, they direct, but most of all they mentor and help navigate an extraordinary array of students to that very final point in their studies. His office, as expected, was brimming with books and piles of papers. We chatted about Boston and he gave me a quick lesson in the importance of American football while I, in turn, suggested he needed to see some Aussie Rules Football. But time was precious and we moved on to the topic of the vandalism.

On the night of Tuesday 17 November 2015, the black and white portrait photographs of some of the African American Harvard Law School professors and lecturers had been struck across with black tape. There were no security cameras and no alarm appears to have been raised. On the following Wednesday morning, Professor Sullivan walked into Wasserstein Hall in the direction of his lecture theatre and was shocked to see his defaced portrait. His portrait is hard to miss. It is prominently placed among the ground-floor row of portraits that extend the length of the building and is located near one of the larger lecture theatres. He cast aside his initial response and gave his lecture; he downgraded the defacing to the level of some kind of prank and chose to try to ignore it.

But his attempt to discount the act of vandalism was not going to be easy. His students were devastated and, as their teacher, he realised he needed to provide direction on how to deal with the defacement. He placated them and advised they should move on as he had. Yet the image of the portrait with the black tape across his eyes was startling. How did he feel given that this was his domain, his space as a teacher? His response was gradually one of anger. 'Was that meant to be some kind of attempt to stop me interacting in the world?' he asked. If this was meant to stop him, this act of blocking him out, then whoever did this was mistaken. Professor Sullivan's ire was clearly still evident as we discussed the incident.

His students were generally upset, others were embarrassed, perhaps assuming that a student group had enacted the crime (the police treated the matter as a hate crime), but it was particularly his black students who were the most concerned for the African American professoriate. They were, indeed, protective of their mentors, whom they see as representative of a desired career, lifestyle and measure of achievement. They see their future reflected in Professor Sullivan and his colleagues. His achievement is mighty from any perspective: not only is he the first African American ever appointed Faculty Dean at Harvard, but he also has a most esteemed career working to free wrongly convicted criminals, with persons who had served up to thirty years in prison exonerated through his advocacy. Yet his experience at Harvard left him perplexed at the vandalism of the portraits. The impetus for the action in the confines of a place that is regarded as offering the space to debate and explore was disturbing. 'How far have we really come?' he asked.

According to writer Martin Gayford, the British have resisted the opportunity to be 'statue-conscious' in relation to honouring past politicians and other notables from history, Nelson on his column being one of the few examples.[12] There is, however, the statue of Henry VIII at St Bartholomew's Hospital, a strange place to display the likeness of a man who willingly executed whole families to prevent any claims to the throne (Henry Pole and family through their relationship to the last York kings), as well as past wives and supposed adulterers (Mark Smeaton, famously executed as one of many charged with adultery in relation to Queen Anne Boleyn), or simply those who were inconvenient. Some put the number of executions in the thousands.

There is the statue of Cecil Rhodes at Oxford University that remains in spite of a call for its toppling due to Rhodes' association with the introduction of segregation in southern Africa. There are the statues of the first Governor of the penal colony of New South Wales,

Admiral Arthur Phillip, in Watling Street near St Paul's Cathedral and another in St Mary-le-Bow Church. Phillip enacted the orders of the British Government to govern the First Fleet of convicts at the settlement at Sydney Cove and ensure the Indigenous people did not hinder the establishment of that settlement.

There is also the equestrian statue of Charles I located at Charing Cross, which boasts quite an extraordinary history. Following the English Civil War and the beheading of Charles I in 1649, his statues were set upon with singular ferocity, and many of them succumbed to destruction. Luckily for the equestrian statue of Charles I by Hubert Le Sueur, there was a metalsmith by the name of John Rivet who had purchased the statue and, in spite of being ordered by Parliament to completely destroy the work, buried the statue until the Restoration in 1660, pretending that pieces of broken brass were from the horse. He did rather well from the sale of brass-handled knives and forks, purchased by Royalists as sacred relics. When the statue was finally found, it was written that it had been 'exhumed from its concealment', and when placed at Charing Cross it was honoured poetically: 'That the First Charles does here in triumph ride' – extraordinary language for a statue.[13]

There are, of course, statues of Governor Arthur Phillip in Australia along with representations of many other early Governors including Lachlan Macquarie – the Governor responsible for shooting parties who included in their actions the Appin massacre of Aboriginal Australians on 17 April 1816.[14] In Sydney's Hyde Park, an area originally set aside by Governor Phillip in 1792, a statue of the voyager Captain Cook towers over visitors and workers as they pass by to seek the shade of the Moreton Bay fig trees and escape the humid midday heat. The statue is typical of the nineteenth-century approach to portrayal, a gloriously heroic image of the explorer who stands with his arm outstretched and poised as though he were about to be handed the world. There is a plaque beneath the statue upon which is written 'Discovered this Territory 1770'. While Cook explored and charted the east coast of Australia and claimed it for the British Empire, he did not discover Australia. Perhaps inspired by protests around the world to the reminders of a colonialist past, the statue of Cook was vandalised in August 2017 with the graffiti 'No Pride in Genocide' and 'Change the Date' written upon the stone plinth on which it stands. Other statues of Cook have often been plastered with paint in a similar statement regarding the need for recognition of Australia's First Peoples [Figure 21].

In response, the former Prime Minister of Australia, Malcolm Turnbull, wrote on his Facebook page:

> This is what Stalin did. When he fell out with his henchmen he didn't just execute them, they were removed from all official photographs – they became non-persons, banished not just from life's mortal coil but from memory and history itself.[15]

It is a charged response to a request for the wording of the plaque to be changed to state that Cook claimed the territory for the British Empire and that it should include recognition of the rights of the First Peoples. The statue, by its very nature, reminds some members of the public of the impact of Cook's 'discovery' of Australia. The artist Vernon Ah Kee of the Kuku Yalandji, Waanji, Yidinji and Gugu Yimithirr people summarises the history he was taught as follows:

> It's so wildly out of context that it renders me as a person invisible, invalid, unrecognizable, not real at all . . . That's how this culture accepts Aboriginal people.[16]

The official response to the damage to Captain Cook's statue is a marked contrast to the commentary on the vandalising of the West Australian statue of Noongar man Mokare. Explorers relied heavily upon Aboriginal people to help in the tracking of country in order to draw the maps of Australia. They also depended upon Aboriginal knowledge of survival in the Australian bush. One such Aboriginal tracker was Mokare, well known in the region that includes what is now the town of Albany. Mokare worked with the white men exploring and navigating the western region. It was a strategy adopted by many Aboriginal communities to reduce the threat of the gun-carrying white settlers.

Mokare accompanied visitors such as the explorer Major Edmund Lockyer along his Noongar walking tracks in 1827, effectively showing him the way into his country. It is intrinsic to Indigenous culture to work to protect and sustain areas of land required for food and shelter and so Mokare peaceably worked with the new arrivals to ensure survival of his community.[17]

Mokare also worked with the government resident and surgeon Dr Alexander Collie to explore areas of the southwest. When Collie died in 1835, four years after Mokare, he asked to be buried by his side. Collie's contribution to settlement and exploration resulted in a town named in his honour along with a river, a street in Perth and the erection of a monument in 1935. The town of Albany came out to attend the funeral of Mokare in 1831; in 1978 a park in Albany was finally named in his honour, and then a reconciliation project in 1997 resulted in a statue erected to commemorate his desire for peaceful relations. An attempt to harm that statue occurred in 2012 when it was painted white. There was an outcry from the local Indigenous community; the Mayor of Albany commented, but the wider population including Federal politicians remained silent.

Australia's history remains a contested site. While the date of arrival of Indigenous people shifts as further investigations are undertaken, it is believed their heritage and occupation of Australia can be traced back 65,000 years. Yet the relationship between the Indigenous people and the colonisers who acted under the banner of the expansionist policies of the British Empire could be written in one word: catastrophic. As Cook set foot on the land and ordered the firing of the first musket at the Indigenous people, fearful that the spears pointed at him were poisoned, he set in motion a behaviour of antagonism towards, and ignorance of, Indigenous Australians. The right to declare ownership of land that had not been declared by any other powerful white nation was acceptable during the Age of Enlightenment. Considered a fine navigator, Captain Cook had been charged with finding the Great South Land, a search that had confounded explorers hitherto or, in the case of the Dutch, not been of any great interest.

On the long, arduous journey that tested his nerve as Captain as well as his crew's tenacity, Cook carried with him secret instructions administered by the Admiralty that specified the right to claim the land, but only after negotiation: 'You are also with the Consent of the Natives to take Possession of Convenient Situations in the Country in the Name of the King of Great Britain: Or: if you find the Country uninhabited take Possession for his Majesty ...'[18] The instructions were in keeping with the then-recent adjustment of British imperialism toward a tempered observance and respect for Native American and Maori communities. Within the pages of Cook's journals, it is possible to work through the reasoning that led to his claiming of the eastern coast of the Great South Land for the British Empire. His grounds for such a claim were manifold but included his observations that the numbers of the natives were so low as not to be considered as occupiers; that they did not undertake any associated agriculture; and that they appeared decidedly primitive.

Having arrived upon Possession Island, Cape York, on 22 August 1770, Cook chose at this moment in his journey to claim in the name of King George III the whole eastern coast of Australia on the basis that the continent was effectively *terra nullius*, i.e. without occupation. It was the same King George III, wearing a Roman toga, whose gilded equestrian statue in Bowling Green, a park in Manhattan, was unceremoniously pulled to the ground by a mob upon the reading of the Declaration of Independence to New Yorkers in 1776. In order to convey the significance of the tearing down of the statue, a replica has been placed on display at the Museum of the American Revolution in Philadelphia.

Cook was, of course, wrong in his assessment that there was no governance of the land, communication across the land or management of the sustainability of the land by its Indigenous population. Research of early settlers and ethnographers' journals has shown that they were, indeed, surprised and in some cases disturbed to learn that many Indigenous people understood the geography across the continent as well as kept data on sea level rises, among other knowledge of country.[19] Today, the Australian people have a much deeper understanding of country and the meaning of country for Indigenous people.

Debate over the nature of British colonisation of Australia, the dispossession and ultimate annihilation of many clans of Indigenous Australians, as well as the teaching of Australian history and its impact upon racist behaviour have formed the basis of what are known in Australia as the history wars. They play into notions of contemporary identity which should, of course, be a site of continual adjustment and scrutiny. Perhaps the activities of colonisation can best be placed in context through the words and actions of John Batman, who described the shooting of Tasmanian Aboriginals in 1829.

Batman is traditionally considered Melbourne's 'founding father' due to a negotiated treaty with Wurundjeri elders in 1835, a treaty that due to language differences and indistinct concepts of ownership is not a valid document (in addition to Batman's lack of Crown authority to undertake any negotiation). Prior to his arrival in Melbourne, Batman lived in Tasmania when, as leader of a roving party to pursue those who had been committing 'outrages' in the district, he and his party ambushed a tribe and upon their running into the bush, he recalled, 'I ordered the men to fire upon them, which was done'. Batman took prisoner a woman, child and two wounded men, one with an ankle injury. Twelve others had been severely injured and, it was presumed, were dead or dying but had managed to crawl away into the bush. The Batman party left the shooting site with a cache of spears, knives and:

> with the two men, woman and child, but found it impossible that the two former could walk, and after trying them by every means in my power, for some time, found I could not get them on I was obliged to shoot them.[20]

The woman was sent to jail; Batman kept the child.

A statue of Batman, unveiled in 1979 at a site in the heart of Melbourne, has recently been removed as a result of a property development, and its future location is under discussion. The statue raises similar issues as those for the Harvard Law School shield.

A major opponent to the removal of the shield was Harvard legal historian Annette Gordon-Reed who argued that the presence of the shield reminded people of the slave history and could be a strategy of memory association that should be accompanied by a narrative context. Equally, it has been argued by Wemba Wemba-Wergaia historian Dean Stewart that to keep the Batman statue ensures that it can act as a pivot to telling the story of Batman's slaughter of Tasmanian Aboriginals and the treaty he made with the Wurundjeri people, stripping them of their land and rights.[21]

Anthropologists in the nineteenth century rushed to Australia to observe the Indigenous people before the prophecies of Darwinian evolutionary theories saw the predicted demise of the Aboriginal. Researchers such as Baldwin Spencer and F.J. Gillen travelled to Central Australia to observe the Arrernte people within the context of their Social Darwinism principles, i.e. the strength of white society is enhanced through the demise of a lesser race. Yet the contested site of such principles gives way to a note of humanism in their observations, that they were concerned 'as best [they] could to enter into the feelings, to think as they did, and to become for the time being one of themselves'.[22]

The presence of anthropologists exemplifies the dichotomy of existence for mainland Aboriginal people. The research was able to distinguish the complexity of custom, locate the cultural artefacts and the extraordinary paintings on rock faces, and discern some knowledge of spiritual life. It assisted in providing a measure of the structure of Indigenous Australian society, of the importance of family and custom.

Portraits of Indigenous Australians in the late eighteenth and nineteenth centuries were manipulated, Europeanised, rejected, idealised, characterised and taken from the heads retrieved from massacred bodies. The increased interest in the appearance of the native people of Australia was due in large part to the 1795 publication of Johann Blumenbach's *De Generis Humani Varietate Nativa,* which established a desire among European scientists for skulls that could assist with their theories on the origins of man.[23] Sir Joseph Banks, the botanist who accompanied Captain Cook on the journey of the *Endeavour* to the south Pacific Ocean, was later instrumental in securing Aboriginal skulls for Blumenbach to work from, and he is duly credited on the cover of the 1795 publication.

The impact of contemporary theories of evolution meant that many portrait artists of Indigenous Australians at the turn of the century had the same offensive objective as the artists portraying Native Americans – to depict the race before it was extinct. In both cases it was not the portraits that were destroyed – it was presumed to be the people. Indigenous subjects from both continents were prey to the imaging by artists and photographers who played with the notion of identity as a means to illustrate contemporary views of persistence and evolution. Just as the dominant culture had destroyed rights to country, so the portrait became a contested site of survival. The portrait artist of the Indigenous subject was often less interested in personality and far more interested in a typical view that could garner income from the delivery of an image that illustrated an ethnographic theory.

Theorist Hans-Georg Gadamer provides guidance on the notion of the use of the portrait for means other than to convey the individual identity of the subject. The individual, he argued, was always present in a portrait, and the desire to provide an idealisation:

> does not alter the fact that a portrait represents an individual, and not a type, however much a portrait may transform the person portrayed from the incidental and the private into the essential, the true appearance.[24]

Due to the desire to often convey a type in portraits of Indigenous peoples, it is easy to associate all portraiture from the era of nineteenth-century ethnographic study with type, i.e. if the image is of a dark-skinned person it must be for scientific or social purposes. An alternative view is evident in the portrait of a Bundjalung woman by the nineteenth-century Australian artist Tom Roberts (*Portrait of an Aboriginal Woman [Maria Yulgilbar]*, 1895; State Library of NSW, Sydney). Roberts depicts her quiet contemplation, his sensitive observation providing the space for her authority to be realised and confirm the work as a portrait, i.e. it reflects the life as portrayed before the artist and subsequently the viewer. It is possible to consider Maria Yulgilbar's place in the world, and indeed her measure of the world around her is communicated through her sense of belonging.

The portrait by Roberts contrasts with the nineteenth-century images of Indigenous Australians in which subjects are literally smothered by the idealisation that was often the by-product of commercial concerns of publishers. The portraits were part of the positive propaganda of the image of the new colony. For the 1789 publication *The Voyage of Governor Phillip to Botany Bay*, the drawings were not the originals submitted with the text. The publishers had been disappointed with the honesty of the depiction of the Indigenous people and made the decision that the drawings might detract from the aesthetics of the book, and so they were rejected. The volumes dedicated to voyages of discovery in the Pacific region in the late eighteenth century were traditionally investments in grand, beautifully coloured, quarto-size productions designed to 'interest virtuosi and men of taste for whom the image of the native as a noble savage still held a strong quasi-aesthetic appeal'.[25] Taste played a great part in what was included.

Historian Bernard Smith investigated the illustrations in Phillip's *Voyage* and deduced that they were not the drawings sent to London from Sydney but were 'neo-classical prototypes of the noble savage' that can also be seen in the publications associated with Cook's voyages.[26] As Smith has investigated, the artists responsible for the drawings are unknown; an artist to accompany the First Fleet was not considered relevant.

An artist did accompany Matthew Flinders on the sloop *Investigator* as it charted the Australian coast in 1801. William Westall, a student at the Royal Academy, engaged fully in the opportunity and spent considerable time on the mainland producing visual documents of his interactions. His commitment to a direct portrayal of the people he met can be discerned in his 1802 drawing *Port Jackson: A Native (no. 1)*, now at the National Library of Australia, Canberra, which exhibits a close interaction with the subject. His portraits as described by Elisabeth Findlay are 'filled with melancholy ... and understanding beyond the stereotyped noble savage images he was producing for the Admiralty'.[27] The Admiralty, a government department directed by five lords commissioners, provided orders for the navy and had ultimate responsibility and ownership of any material emanating from a voyage. Unfortunately, Westall's portraits were not published in their original state.

Westall had shown a keen interest in the lives and customs of the mainland Aboriginal people and his sensitivity to their plight and treatment can be observed in his work. Yet he was only nineteen years of age and, without any experience of the many vagaries of such a voyage, complained to Sir Joseph Banks at the lack of interesting subject matter to be found in 'New Holland'. He was angling for alternative pastures and requested that he receive support to travel to India 'as compensation'. Banks had little patience for such complaints and Westall was ultimately sacked and told to find his own way home. All of the surviving sketches and watercolours were delivered to London as per the contract, but due to Flinders' incarceration on Mauritius for seven years, the material was left to gather dust.

Eventually the Admiralty asked Westall to work up the sketches into nine oil paintings, works that could best be described as picturesque fabrications of serene moments in the life of the colony.

In 2013, I travelled to the Torres Strait Islands to effectively retrace something of the artist Tom Roberts' journey aboard a pearling lugger in 1892. I was hoping to discover what had inspired Roberts to leave the freedom of his bohemian existence in a community of men living in view of Sydney Harbour, sign up as a deckhand on the *Jessie* for the princely sum of a shilling, work alongside the pearl fishers and spend two months in a region unknown to him. In 1892, Roberts was emerging as a significant portrait artist alongside his more popular work producing iconic paintings of life in the Australian bush. For my journey, there were no nineteenth-century pearling luggers available, so I travelled as a passenger on a freight ship leaving from Cairns, heading up along the extraordinary coast of northeastern Australia and through the treacherous Great Barrier Reef. It was a route that had brought many voyagers to grief, including Captain Cook, whose ship foundered on the reef he named Endeavour Reef; and Matthew Flinders on an attempted voyage to England in 1803.

The vegetation along the northern coastline shows little sign of encroachment from development and few signs of life except for small boats and campers. We were about twenty passengers in all, braving the rain on deck one afternoon to observe Cape York, the northernmost tip of Australia. The coast that day lacked the roar of the surf Cook had observed when he sailed past in 1770. From this geographic and historic marker that harbours the stories of the lives of so many people, we headed directly for the Torres Strait Islands. I disembarked at Thursday Island, the central island.

Roberts painted a number of portraits while travelling through the Torres Strait Islands, his journey guided by former Premier of Queensland John Douglas and his aides – and accompanied at times by the botanical painter Ellis Rowan. Roberts contributed a four-part travelogue to the *Argus* of his experiences sailing through the islands as well as his involvement in local customs and ceremonies. Yet it is his vivid narrative of the very public painting of a portrait of a local man called Dao on Mer (Murray) Island that provides an insight into the local community. The painting became a performance, with the Islander communities gathering on the beach to watch as the image evolved. Dao was described by Roberts as 'having a fine, strongly marked face and a half-sad, half-wild expression'. He scarcely stirred for two and a half hours during the painting process, the surrounding crowd applauding at pivotal moments:

> when a high light on the bronzey nose goes in the applause rises; the crowd follows every touch of the brush, and when there comes in a tuft of white hair characteristic of the subject there is a roar, a grin all round.[28]

Ellis Rowan describes what occurred next.

Then as the boy's friends pressed around them and Roberts was putting the finishing touches to the picture, it fell, 'Butter side downwards' into the sand. It looked hopeless, but next day the oils had dried and we carefully wiped off the sand, after which it was retouched and looked as well as ever.[29]

It was almost a portrait destroyed – although, as the picture does not seem to have survived after all, Roberts may very well have decided that it was as good as destroyed with its embedded sand and smudged features.

Some might conjecture that it was a fitting end. While Roberts had spent a considerable number of years travelling throughout Australia and depicting the scenes and people he encountered, there remains the question of authority to represent identity, stories and history of another cultural group.

A work that did survive and that delineates the relevance of portraiture to family, identity and memory is the sketch portrait by Roberts of Dick Rotumah, also completed while Roberts was on Mer Island [Figure 22]. Rotumah was a pearl diver, one of the most dangerous professions at that time. The portrait presents Rotumah as the stockman rather than the diver, with his soft-brimmed hat and open-neck shirt. He scrutinises the artist warily, and we can imagine

Roberts sitting before him, drawing his features using only the few simple lines that make up the portrait.

The story of the portrait and its contemporary significance as a personal memento highlight the nature of portraiture and its power to connect across generations. On my journey to the Torres Strait Islands it was on Mer Island that I had chosen to spend the majority of my time. Roberts had travelled to the island and remained there for some days, painting and watching the cultural life and ceremony. I had received permission from the Torres Strait Island Regional Council to visit Mer Island and boarded a commuter plane to make the journey from Horn Island. Others on the plane were returning home, visiting relatives or travelling to provide services to the islands. A man seated in front of me was intrigued by my presence, guests from Melbourne a rarity. I told him of my research into the portraits by Tom Roberts and his face lit up. 'I have one,' he replied.

A short stop at Yorke Island provided the opportunity to ask further details. Father Dalton Cowley is the local Anglican priest, working across the islands but mostly based at the Tagai State College on Mer Island. Father Cowley explained that he had a copy of Roberts' portrait of Dick Rotumah, which had kindly been provided to him by the Mitchell Library. He is a fifth-generation descendant of Rotumah, who, along with many islander men in the nineteenth century, had sought the riches of the pearl shell (bêche-de-mer) industry and journeyed from Rotuma Island, which lies to the north near New Guinea. Dick Rotumah tragically died from paralysis caused by diving in 1911, nineteen years after Roberts had sketched his portrait. He must have been an extremely fit man given that he was forty-three years of age when he died – old to be diving to the dangerous ten to fifteen fathom depths of the ocean to find the sought-after pearl shells. His middle name was Cedric, and it is after Dick Rotumah that the Cedric Passage is named.[30]

The next day Father Cowley showed me the portrait – a copy of Roberts' quiet study of Dick Rotumah – the resemblance uncanny across generations. He also had a family photograph of three of the generations: Dick and his partner, Mogi, had a daughter named Linnie, who was pictured along with her son and granddaughter, who was Father Cowley's mother. The portrait of Dick Rotumah provides the connection for Father Cowley not only to his ancestor but to the contested heritage and ownership of the Torres Strait Island land.

Mer Island is creole in language and culture, its location in the Pacific Ocean among Melanesian countries such as Papua New Guinea and the Solomon Islands differentiating its people from the mainland Aboriginal clans. My nights there were spent listening to the reggae music that would filter through the cool night from surrounding houses, the salty air of the great Pacific Ocean and sounds of the island so poignant. The island was also the home of Eddie Koiki Mabo, the former pearl diver, teacher's aide, Indigenous rights advocate and university gardener who, upon learning that the Crown owned the lands upon which his people lived, chose to fight for his birthright to own his home.

His stance resulted in a landmark case whereby the High Court of Australia ruled in *Mabo and Others v Queensland (No. 2)* that the doctrine of *terra nullius*, the doctrine upon which the British had claimed the right to import laws and claim ownership, did not apply on Mer Island. The reasons were embedded in the life of the Indigenous population, which had a pre-existing system of law and a sustained connection to the land under traditional laws and customs; essentially, it meant that native title for Mer Island was sustained. Unfortunately, Mabo died five months prior to the decision on 3 June 1992.

I had met Eddie Mabo's cousin Annie when I arrived at the Mer Island accommodation; she had helped me settle into the large council house that was my lodging for the three days. She explained that when Eddie's mother died soon after giving birth, he was adopted by his mother's brother, as is islander tradition, his father asking that he be taught to protect the land.

Three years after the High Court decision, the Mabo family chose to commemorate Eddie Mabo's death with the unveiling of his tombstone in the Townsville cemetery and to bring the community together with a traditional feast. This was an important moment for the family as it signified that the period of mourning was over and Eddie Mabo's spirit had been given the final appropriate passage to the afterlife. The black marble headstone was decorated with a statement that told the story of his fight for justice while his totems (symbols of his identity), the shark and the Torres Strait pigeon, were engraved on either side of his smiling bronze face that emerged from the black marble. It is believed that while the evening feast took place, desecration of Mabo's grave occurred. Red swastikas and abusive words were scrawled across the granite, but it was the unbolting and taking away of Mabo's heroic joyous face from its position in the centre of the tombstone that shocked Australian people.[31]

Mabo was symbolically beheaded – the attack racist and debilitating. It was a message that paid reference to the historical relationship; this is what had happened to Indigenous people when they fought against the landing and resettlement of British people according to British colonial policy, and it was the heads of Indigenous people sent to Europe for the study of evolutionary theory. While the Torres Strait Islanders had been largely protected from the major acts of violence and dispossession of land, they did suffer losses, had been exploited by the pearling industry, had encountered the white diseases and had been placed under the control of the Queensland government. From the age of twenty-one Eddie Mabo commenced his political activism, advocating for his fellow Torres Strait Islanders who worked on the railways in Cairns. From that moment, his body was a political body and he employed the terms of argument, evidence and desire that belonged to the white governing hierarchy. He hoped to ensure the sustainability of his culture, his language and its principles and this became a pivotal objective of his work.

Australia came together in its condemnation of the desecration of the grave. Few Indigenous issues had mattered so profoundly. The destruction of the bronze portrait was considered another blow for Indigenous people – as though it were a living being. All sides of the political spectrum offered support, funds and assistance to remove Mabo's grave from its site of desecration and place it in the protected confines of Mer Island. The armed forces offered to help transport the body and casket to the remote island. It became an act of penance; the wrongs of the past that destroyed the bodies of Indigenous people could not be rectified, there would still be disagreement over the massacres, any claim for native title would still need to be ratified through the court system, but if the body of Mabo could be protected and a new portrait bust produced, then the country could calmly feel that one soul had received a collective embrace.

Eddie Mabo has become a significant figure in the history of Australian law and human rights. When the mural on the side of the Uniting Church's Wayside Chapel in Bondi, New South Wales, was commissioned and painted in 2013, a collaboration between Wiradjuri man Paul Davis and British Australian naïve artist Etienne Cohen, Mabo's portrait was included as one of five respected Indigenous people who had contributed to the Australian community [Figure 23]. Children from Goodooga, a remote town in New South Wales, who had never before seen the sea visited Bondi to see the mural, dipped their hands in paint and symbolically connected to those who had fought for recognition, indeed for their future.

The emergence of contemporary Indigenous artists in the latter part of the twentieth century has resulted in ownership of the imaging of experience, expression of views that absorb and analyse mainstream readings of history and occupation, and a self-expression that enlightens and identifies the relationships with the dominant culture. Unfortunately, the community around the mural learnt in 2016 that there was to be an internal redevelopment of the Chapel and while it was understood the mural wall was to remain, the mural needed to be destroyed. There was a campaign to save the mural and applications were made to the local Waverley Council. They asked for more time to gather information and to make a heritage application. This was denied.

With the community campaign growing in momentum and the media taking an interest in the artwork, which they saw as a political and social issue, it was disturbing that the Uniting Church painted over the mural on 30 November 2016. It was – to use a term that can readily be applied to the treatment of Indigenous Australians in general – a whitewash.

The mural that the Church painted over contained the portraits of Vincent Lingiari, Mum Shirl Smith, Eddie Mabo, Faith Bandler and Charles Perkins, all activists and workers for their community. The community had undertaken the series of permissions required for the public display of the images of all five people. In Indigenous culture, the family must give permission for an image to be displayed and for a name to be spoken in the immediate period after someone's death. Though considerable time had passed, the portraits were to be placed so prominently that the community decided it best to ensure the cultural process was respected.

The mural painters had chosen their subjects well. Vincent Lingiari, a man of the Gurindji people, led the famous 1966 walk-off of stockmen, house maids and families from the Northern Territory Wave Hill cattle station owned by Vesteys. They had been 'treated like dogs' by the management, they proclaimed, but not only did they want humane conditions of employment, they also wanted their land. The protest lasted for nine years, during which time Lingiari toured Australia and spoke of his rights. A partial handback of land was negotiated and announced on Gurindji country by Prime Minister Gough Whitlam in 1975. A poignant photograph by Mervyn Bishop of Lingiari poised as Whitlam pours pure, fine dirt into his wrinkled, cupped hand has become an iconic image of the changed views towards land rights. Lingiari chuckles and looks into his hand as the familiar dirt falls, while Whitlam, a most impressive figure, appears proud of the progress on the issue.[32]

Both Mum Shirl Smith and Faith Bandler were activists for Aboriginal rights; Faith Bandler campaigned for the 1967 referendum that provided for Indigenous Australians to be included in the population census and for the Federal Government to legislate specifically for their rights. Smith devoted her life to helping reunite children with their families and found a series of organisations to provide support in areas such as legal and medical services. Charles Perkins was also involved in the 1967 referendum campaign and later became Permanent Secretary of the Department of Aboriginal Affairs – a first for an Indigenous man.

The four portraits were placed beside that of Eddie Mabo, the images an inspiration for the community and a site of learning about the struggle for basic human rights for Indigenous people. Australian copyright law protects the integrity of the artist, including that any derogatory treatment or destruction needs to have the permission of the artist. The grandson of Mum Shirl Smith commented that the destruction of the portrait was akin to attending her funeral all over again, 'with tears rolling down all our faces while the painter was there covering the rest of the picture'.[33]

CHAPTER 7

Artists Destroy
and Destroyed

There are works we hope are not destroyed. Benjamin Duterrau's group portrait, the 5-metre-long *The National Picture* (c.1840), has been missing and presumed destroyed since the nineteenth century. It portrays the government-appointed 'Protector of Aborigines', George Augustus Robinson, posed with an unidentified group of Tasmanian Aboriginals. Robinson coordinated the relocation program of removing the Tasmanian Aboriginals from Tasmania to a settlement on Flinders Island. Whereas there was a population of over four thousand Tasmanian Aboriginals prior to white settlement, it is thought that only approximately a hundred and fifty remained by 1835.

Duterrau, an artist who travelled from London in 1832 to set up his painting studio in Hobart, also produced the companion piece *The Conciliation* (1840; Tasmanian Museum and Art Gallery,

Hobart), thought to be a sketch for the larger *The National Picture*. While some of the people portrayed in this sketch are identified, it is unclear if their portraits were transferred to the larger picture that is now lost. Duterrau's portraiture of Tasmanian Aboriginals remains an area of conflict, the portrayal considered by some a sympathetic observance of the plight of First Peoples, while others consider the portraits as facilitators of the views of racial extinction. The work of the artist is now scrutinised within a context of ownership of image; for example, historian Amy Tritton explores the association between Duterrau and a number of the subjects of his portraits. She proposes that the Aboriginal people pictured actually requested the portraits to be painted, effectively commissioning the works, having developed good relationships with Duterrau.[1]

Finding *The National Picture* was the holy grail of a worldwide search by Stephen Scheding, and while he was able to confirm that the picture did exist at one time, it remains lost or destroyed.[2] He tracked it to a house in Scotland, but there the search ended; the significant size of the painting meant it would not be easily hidden. Throughout his search and following the publication of his book detailing the search, Scheding received substantial attention in the press both in Britain and Australia but, to date, no one has come forward with details of its whereabouts. The common theory is that the work was either cut down or possibly completely destroyed. The historical importance of the picture – the claim that it is the first (white) history picture in Australia – means the work has lived on, commonly appropriated as a means to engage with colonialist assimilation and 'civilising' policies in which Duterrau, through the staging of the group portrait, was complicit. Maulboyheenner (Timmy), the central character of *The Conciliation*, was hanged in 1842 – one of the first people, along with his friend Tunnerminnerwait, to be hanged in Melbourne.

The nineteenth-century bohemian life of the French artists who heralded the age of Impressionism was teeming with envy, power and extraordinary talent. To compete, an artist had to bring a measure of genius and an ego capable of countering the most blistering critiques. Yet reproach was also at the instigation of one's friends. Édouard Manet, reeling from the response to his *Olympia* (1863; Musée d'Orsay, Paris), could hardly have been comforted by the words of Charles Baudelaire. 'You, by contrast, are merely the finest painter in the decrepitude of your art,' he replied to Manet on 11 May 1865, not long after *Olympia* was exhibited at the Paris Salon.[3]

Manet was angry at the continual attacks upon his work. Guards had been required to ensure threatening knives had not slashed his painting of the artist and his mistress, Victorine Meurent, posed as Olympia. A dislike of the hierarchy that controlled the Parisian art world resulted in Manet mounting a private exhibition in 1867. Yet the poor reviews and public response continued, and Manet battled his demons of self-doubt concurrently with his expectations of demonstrations of public acknowledgement.

In 1868, it was either artistic redress, jealousy or love of his wife that was at the heart of Manet's famous slashing from top to bottom and subsequent removal of a third of a domestic portrait by Edgar

Degas. The cutting struck right through the face and body of Madame Suzanne Manet, brutal in its assault. It was a double portrait of the couple. Suzanne is seated on a chair, her finely crafted, elegant white muslin and black-ribboned dress spilling around the seat, her hair wound into a bountiful chignon. The remnant of her body suggests she is poised as though at a piano, her abilities the centre of attention, while Manet slumps uncomfortably on a cream settee as though he has eaten too profoundly at Sunday lunch. He is inattentive to his wife, stares vacantly into the distance, their connection only rescued by Manet's foot hidden beneath his wife's dress. This is all that remains of the composition of *Monsieur and Madame Édouard Manet* (1868–69; Kitakyushu Municipal Museum of Art, Japan).

Degas had presented the portrait to Manet in the act of exchange of pictures that often occurs between artists. They had met approximately six years earlier in the Louvre, Manet noticing Degas as he undertook a copy of Velázquez's *Infanta Maria Margarita* (1653), she the central figure of *Las Meninas*. Manet, a couple of years older, introduced Degas to his circle of friends, and it was from Manet that Degas often received advice.

According to Auguste Renoir, they were on good terms, although their friendship 'was not without frequent quarrels and reconciliations'.[4] Such an ability to continue the friendship in spite of creative differences locates Manet's action as even more perplexing. To undertake such permanent destruction of a work is confounding – he could have simply returned the picture to the artist, just as Degas returned Manet's small still life of plums to him following one of their many quarrels.

Degas demanded the return of his portrait of the Manets declaring that he would fix the picture but never attempted the repair – although a blank piece of canvas was added to the torn canvas. He kept the picture as a reminder to be wary of his friend and artistic rival. Renoir was guarded in his praise of Manet's originality, believing that Degas gave Manet the theme for an 1868 portrait he painted of his wife, *Madame Manet at the Piano* (Musée d'Orsay, Paris) – Manet was called by Renoir an 'imitator with genius'.[5] Yet he does his wife no justice; her dress, painted in a deadening black, merges with her chair rather than seductively floating around her body as Degas had observed her. She is flushed and depicted with reddened nose, lost in her reverie and without vanity.

Madame Manet at the Piano is a true portrait of intimacy but painted during a time when Manet was immersed in his affair with Meurent and had recently met the enigmatic artist Berthe Morisot. Indeed, jealousy was not just the domain of Manet. Morisot's mother wrote during this time that Manet was 'at home making a portrait of his wife and laboring to make of that monster something slender and interesting'.[6] Suzanne must have been distraught at the slashing of Degas' portrait and her perfunctory appearance in Manet's version as she plays her beloved piano. She is presented as no longer desirable but rather as she appeared within the routine of their lives. Manet did not wish her to be publicly displayed by another talented, handsome artist in a double portrait.

Women in the nineteenth century were at the mercy of the artists with whom they fraternised, married and posed. They could be portrayed as serenely beautiful, immersed within sunny, floral interiors or gardens of pleasure, their features reconciled to reflect the ambience and beauty. Had Degas strayed into such a space of adoration of Suzanne that upset her husband? It was certainly the unwritten protocol that artists should consider carefully the portrayal of a woman of their desire. Manet did not paint another portrait of Morisot after her marriage to his brother in 1874.[7] He lost a fine model; his portraits of Morisot are deeply personal and resonate with the hint of intimacy that defined their close relationship. Realism promoted a truth to appearance and portrayal in a sincere manner. Manet sought truth in his many portraits and subject pictures, his few surviving self-portraits suggesting he preferred to place others within his gaze.

Manet was conflicted in his many portraits of Suzanne, as evidenced in a portrait he commenced possibly in 1848, worked on in the mid-1860s, but that was not completed until 1873: his *La Lecture* (Musée d'Orsay, Paris). It traverses the time of their first meeting, the controversies surrounding Manet's salon pictures and their relationship. He portrays Suzanne in a soft white gown, frilled sleeves and black belt across her waist, the sun filtering through the window upon her face, her dress merging with the equally pale settee. Behind her, Manet later painted Léon, her son, reading. The complexity of the intervening years, the trauma over the reception of his work, the guilt over the slashing of Degas' portrait, fighting in the Franco-Prussian War and the many affairs had perhaps led him to seek forgiveness from Suzanne in the form of this portrait. Léon's parentage has been the subject of much speculation: he was publicly acknowledged as Suzanne's younger brother, but there is also evidence that he is the son of Manet's father; Suzanne worked as the music teacher for the Manet family prior to her marriage to Manet.

The impetus for one artist to so violently attack the work of another must be rooted in a complexity of emotions and loyalty. Artists rely on one another's camaraderie for protection and support, most particularly in an environment of avant-garde practice. Manet did not destroy the portrait Degas had painted of him, obviously liking the image of his thoughtful character. It diverged from the clean and elegant portraits of Manet painted by Henri Fantin-Latour, in which Manet is posed as a member of the bourgeois elite in top hat and cane. Degas was interested in the layer beneath such masquerade, and he found his image of Manet in the lounging figure on a couch, a figure who clearly felt at ease in the company of his friend. Unfortunately, the artist depicted had a very firm view of his public image and any double portraits were at his behest; his early *La Pêche* (1862–63; Metropolitan Museum of Art, New York) was a homage to himself and Suzanne, who are both resplendent in Rubenesque costume. They are on the cusp of marriage, Manet attentive to Suzanne. While he may not have completely enjoyed Degas' observance of his meagre attention to his wife while he lay awkwardly across a settee, it is, indeed, interesting that he preserved that side of the portrait.

Vincent Van Gogh painted over portraits he did not like, when his technique had moved forward or when he needed to recycle the canvas. Portraits were a means by which he explored his practice and signified his desire to commit to canvas a view of the ancestors of contemporary society. Prophetic in his perspective, he wrote to his sister in June 1890: 'I should like to paint portraits which would appear after a century to people living then as apparitions'. It is believed one third of his early work hides another work beneath, the assessment made as a result of sophisticated X-ray techniques. One such 1887 work, *Patch of Grass* (Kröller-Müller Museum, Otterlo), a work in which the entire canvas is covered in strokes of green paint, hides a portrait of a woman. The woman is painted in the dark, sombre colours similar to the series of peasant portraits he completed in the mid-eighties, the dramatic change in palette for the overpainting indicative of Van Gogh's artistic progression.

Pablo Picasso, like Van Gogh, was compelled to paint over canvases. The decision tended to be either a result of his work changing, in order to avoid the expense of a new canvas, or possibly even that his opinion of the subject of the portrait had changed. Picasso's *The Blue Room* (1901; The Phillips Collection, Washington, DC) harbours a portrait of a bearded man in evening attire beneath the intimate image of a bathing woman set within a blue-hued bedroom – subject matter commonly found in the work of the French Impressionists. The identity of the man remains unknown, in spite of the use of sophisticated high-spectral scientific equipment to 'see' into the portrait. Scientists have, however, managed to ascertain that the portrait was most likely completed and the paint dry before Picasso embarked on the image of the bathing woman.[8] There is a somewhat sinister element to the looming man's face hidden beneath the woman bathing, particularly in consideration of the painting process.

Picasso painted a traditional head beneath a traditional scene of bathing. The portrait was either painted during or before his Blue Period; the introduction of blue into his work followed the tragic suicide of a friend. Picasso's working method was to see, reduce, deduct and change. It is a process, as Terence Maloon has written, that was predicated on a rejection of first images: 'not only the images provided by perception, but also those given by precedent, by convention, by tradition, and even by his own prior achievements'.[9] His work was profoundly a process of rejection and revolt. His early work provides evidence of the formative stages of developing this sensibility and approach, the traditional portrait beneath *The Blue Room* completely rejected.

The approach to the destruction of a portrait by attacking the body engages with social, political and gender discourse. René Magritte maintained that his 1930 nude portrait of his wife, *The Eternally Obvious* (1948; Metropolitan Museum of Art, New York), was painted as a whole and then cut up into segments and framed, dislocating the parts of the body from one other. Recent analysis has shown that the works were actually individually painted; however, his pretence that he had damaged the portrait was part of the performance of the work, intended to question portrait identity. Is the framed picture of his wife's breasts any more or less a portrait of his wife? Is it necessary to have the framed face with the other segments for it to be considered a portrait? It's tempting to fill in the fictional missing pieces through contemplation of the seen parts, to reconstruct the portrait as complete. Magritte, in typically Surrealist mode, was photographed embracing the work as though the body parts were alive.

Twenty years earlier, František Kupka had reworked a portrait of his wife by painting vertical strokes of colour to almost obliterate her face: the result was *Mme Kupka Among Verticals* (1910–11; Museum of Modern Art, New York). His charge is against figurative painting; his wife appears as though drowning in the colour of his Orphist-style abstraction. Her assigned role within the work was typical of the muse at this time, often unnamed, often the vehicle for the expression of frustrations and desires. When Jacqueline Lamba exhibited her work at the 1935 Surrealist Exhibition, her name was not included. She was also the wife of Surrealist leader André Breton, and was considered within the context of his wife. She destroyed those early works along with works that included portraits from a later exhibition.

It is unclear if it was the artist or subject under attack when the British suffragettes launched their campaign within the museums and galleries in Britain prior to World War I. The finely moulded, elongated back of the National Gallery's *The Toilet of Venus (The Rokeby Venus)*, 1647–51, by Velázquez was hacked by Mary Richardson (Slasher Mary) because it was the most beautiful woman on canvas – but that did not compare to the death of a woman in prison and the appeal of Emmeline Pankhurst. The purpose of the suffragettes was to advocate for basic rights and opportunities for women, and the notoriety to be gained from slashing this picture was too great.

In London in 1914, the suffragettes began to attack portraits of learned and admired men as a means to raise awareness of their cause – rather than attack a living being. On 4 May 1914 Mary Wood (Mary Aldham) famously launched a butcher's cleaver at a portrait of Henry James by John Singer Sargent – as though to slash the portrait would attack authority itself. In his effusive praise of Sargent, James had written that:

> There is no greater work of art than a great portrait – a truth to be constantly taken to heart by a painter holding in his hands the weapon that Mr Sargent wields.[10]

In this case, the weapon held by Wood was violent and capable of destruction. The portrait had been part of the Royal Academy exhibition of that year, the Academy not exactly noted for its support of female painters. In response to the attack, the surrounding visitors set upon a gentleman who was with Wood, but it is the subsequent reaction by the President of the Royal Academy that speaks quite plainly to his hierarchy of values – a portrait by Sargent clearly outstripping the life of a suffragette.

Sir Edward Poynter despised the destructive acts in his gallery carried out by the suffragettes (this was not the first), demanding that rather than having police protect 'the abominable women who commit them from the anger of the crowd', they should consider allowing the crowd to 'give a lesson which would probably make them more careful in future'.[11] His gangland approach to the administering of justice was clearly unsympathetic to Wood's political movement. James' face suffered the greatest impact of the violence, the slash across his mouth indicative of Wood's objection to the authority of the male voice within society, his damaged left eye an attempt to deprive him of his very being.

A similar attack was made by suffragette Anne Hunt upon John Everett Millais' portrait of the writer and philosopher Thomas Carlyle during a visit to the National Portrait Gallery in 1914 [Figure 24]. While these cases are often considered as random attacks (a reasoning that makes the incident far more digestible), in the case of the portrait of Carlyle, it was an attack upon his ideals of literary and philosophical advancement – as well as his role as founder of the National Portrait Gallery. His widely disseminated work *On Heroes and Hero-Worship and the Heroic in History in 1841* had influenced the likes of the photographer Julia Margaret Cameron – her darkly introspective 1867 portrait of Carlyle suggesting that these are spaces she could not tread.[12]

In his writing, Carlyle is pre-eminently of his time, and while he advocated for an adjustment to the obscene prosperity that blessed only a few, he supported the authority of male achievement, strength and wisdom; there was nothing random in Hunt's three blows to the face of Carlyle. In addition, Carlyle believed in the primacy and sincerity of the portrait, that a truly portrayed human being could essentially evoke the memory of that human being. To the suffragettes, attacking the portrait was an attack on male supremacy and the lack of opportunities for women.

Hunt was brazen in both her attack and the defence of her actions. She famously proclaimed at her trial:

> This picture will be of added value and of great historical importance because it has been honoured by the attention of a Militant.[13]

One month after she was released from jail, she returned to the gallery to quietly visit the scene of her actions, much to the shock of the attendant who had been on duty during her smashing and slashing of the picture. But World War I had commenced and her attack upon Carlyle was the last; along with everyone in the community, the suffragettes were far more interested in supporting the war effort.

More recently, the work of the *Artists and Writers Protest Against the War in Vietnam* collective resulted in a body of work that often held the destruction of the portrait as central to the political message of the work. Typical was Carol Summers' large red cross struck across a portrait of a Vietnamese mother and her children, testimony to his anger at life caught within the crossfire. He added perforations to the piece to look like rifle shots and called the work *Kill for Peace*. As Summers usually focused on producing woodcuts of soft-coloured shapes moulded into timeless landscapes, *Kill for Peace* was a dramatic departure. It is indicative of the frustration of such wars that a portrait and its destruction is often the only avenue of opposition.

The artist Francis Bacon destroyed hundreds of works either through the torment of the artistic process, sudden dislike for a subject or simply for entertainment. 'If they were not my friends I could not do such violence to them,' he told David Sylvester in 1966.[14] Bacon often painted purely from memory or used photographs to construct his pictures. It was easier for the artistic process to flow if he was alone with the canvas and his reference material. It also meant that he could avoid enacting his violence towards a picture while a subject was in the room – he would not do that to a friend. Bacon's conversation with Sylvester is about the violence he displayed in the act of painting the canvas – it was intrinsic to his practice of trying to find the source of his subject, to find that element of a character that lurked beneath the façade.

When displeased, Bacon would cut the faces out of portraits to effectively destroy them, often leaving the canvases hanging in the studio for years. Bacon was unable to surround himself with the eyes of those he had failed. Fortunately, the remnants of such acts survive, the hoarded detritus relocated as part of the contents of Bacon's studio to the Dublin City Gallery's 'The Hugh Lane' following Bacon's death. One hundred slashed paintings were found in the studio, either cut by Bacon or his companion, John Edwards, and they are now collected alongside those works that are complete. The missing faces make it impossible to identify some of the portraits, Bacon's objective in keeping the works perhaps grounded in memory and a need to be aware of his fallibility.

Lucian Freud suffered the ignominy of having a portrait destroyed by Bacon. In a moment of indecision, Bacon destroyed his *Portrait of*

George Dyer and Lucian Freud (1967), the picture not making it out of the studio for an upcoming exhibition – but fortuitously, it was photographed. Freud and Bacon had been close friends since the 1940s, and the social quality of their relationship is evident in the portrait. It shows a young Freud somewhat agitated as he perches precariously on a bench, hands tightly clasped as though wishing to be freed from the claustrophobic space that included Bacon's lover. Dyer, the East Ender who had spent far too much time in prison before meeting Bacon, suavely dominates the picture, conversing with both Freud and a person out of view, while Freud is pushed to the edge of the work.

The volatile relationship that defined the interaction between Dyer and Bacon was most likely the cause of the destruction. Or perhaps it was Bacon's sensing that Dyer looked too comfortable. Bacon's preference was for exposure of his subjects rather than allowing them to hide behind a mask of sophistication. In Bacon's paintings of Dyer, prior to this work, he would variously portray him as naked or more sedately in his daily suit, sometimes including both states of appearance in the one portrait. In one picture, Dyer is shown fiercely riding a bike, naked and crouching; in the next, he sits in the middle of the picture contemplating a light bulb. Dyer as the central focus of Bacon's world may have been too much to reconcile and resulted in Bacon's destruction of *Portrait of George Dyer and Lucian Freud.* And, after all, by this time he had painted many portraits of Freud and Dyer – he could live with one fewer.

While Bacon was comfortable with slashing and destroying works, the loss of a portrait did not sit well with Freud. He was, understandably, shocked when he discovered that a commissioned and carefully constructed portrait had been destroyed by a subject. The portrait of the wealthy antiquarian bookseller Bernard Breslauer, painted in the fifties by Freud, was destroyed by Breslauer because, it is said, he didn't like the manner in which Freud had painted his chin. Freud had found Breslauer difficult to engage with and was, apparently, harsher than usual. Freud's portraits were more likely either closely inspected faces as though the very skin of a person would reveal their innermost secrets, or he chose to place subjects against backgrounds that supported the intimacy of their life and achievement in the grand tradition of portraiture. Robert Hughes wrote that Freud's portraits are 'some of the most intensely registered tributes to others in the history of portraiture', an attribute clearly lost on Breslauer.[15]

Breslauer had escaped Nazi Germany for London with his father, Martin, the noted rare-book dealer, and he eventually became a highly respected book dealer in New York. He was accomplished and esteemed within his extremely sophisticated world, and the portrait lacked a consistency of self for Breslauer – this was not how he saw himself. It is difficult to understand that he would consider an ill-conceived chin to have the potential to define him. Or that he felt comfortable destroying an artwork – effectively censoring his image for posterity. Frozen in time within a disagreeable aesthetic was not Breslauer's idea of a future without him. He destroyed the portrait sometime before his death in 2004, clearly not wishing to be remembered according to Freud.

Freud was painstaking in his deliberation over the painting of a portrait. He was known to spend months before he felt satisfied that he had reconciled the identity of the person before him with the image on the canvas. When a small portrait he had painted of Bacon was stolen in 1988 from the Neue Nationalgalerie in Berlin with no clues as to its whereabouts, he decided, thirteen years later, to try to retrieve it. He plastered Berlin with 2500 large 'wanted' posters he had designed as though seeking a long-lost friend [Figure 25].

The portrait of Bacon had been purchased by the Tate gallery soon after Freud had sat with the picture postcard-sized canvas on his knees and painted it in 1951; Bacon was apparently not the most patient of sitters. It was included in a major international touring exhibition of Freud's work organised by the British Council, with the Berlin gallery the last stop on the tour. A reward of DM25,000 for information leading to the whereabouts of the portrait was immediately offered in 1988 following the theft, but no one came forward. In 2001 Freud, still hurt by the theft, participated in the campaign led by the British Council to once again attempt to retrieve the work. The reward this time was DM300,000 and was accompanied by Freud's plea to the perpetrators of the crime that if his painting couldn't be returned, he would be happy to borrow it. In spite of his civil approach (usually public responses are filled with outrage and defiance), there was no return of the painting. He remained hopeful that it belonged to one of the student visitors who came through the gallery on the day it was stolen. The image of the work continues to be included on the Tate gallery website but, in accordance with Freud's wishes, will be reproduced in black and white until the work is found.

Freud mourned the portrait of his close friend, a friend whom – in spite of their sporadically volatile relationship – he treasured. Bacon's death in 1992 enhanced the symbolism of the portrait as a valued connection.[16] The portrait represented for Freud a time past – Bacon's company had entertained him, and their startling and powerful work had shaken the art world – and in spite of everything that had passed between them, they understood the significance of collegiality. It was a symbol also treasured by Bacon who, assisted by his neighbour and friend Barry Joule, apparently attempted to retrieve the portrait after it had been offered to him by 'East End' gangsters in 1989. Bacon was prepared to pay the ransom request of £100,000. He believed the gangsters were unfortunately spooked by police who had been alerted to the deal, and that the portrait had probably been burnt when the exchange fell through.[17] It is unclear if Freud knew of this transaction given his belief that the work remained in Berlin, but perhaps his hope outweighed his consideration of the worst.

Another of Freud's portraits, *Woman with Eyes Closed* (2002), is believed to have been destroyed after it was burnt in the oven of Olga Dogaru. Freud's work was one of a number of portraits by artists including Henri Matisse and Picasso stolen from Rotterdam's Kunsthal museum. Dogaru's son was convicted of stealing the works, while Dogaru was charged with being an accomplice. While she retracted her statement that she burnt the works, fragments were sadly found in her oven, supporting the story of the destruction. While it may be the case that not all works were destroyed (again we live in hope), the completeness of the destruction prompted the judge to fine the thieves the value of the paintings – put at €18 million.

Of course, Dogaru and her son could have returned the pictures anonymously, and the portraits would still be in existence.

Lord Beaverbrook, the enigmatic philanderer, art collector and member of Churchill's inner sanctum, enjoyed his role as the rescuer of the nearly destroyed. When Helena Rubinstein was not exactly enamoured with the 1957 portrait of her by Graham Sutherland, in which she presents with tightly pulled-back hair and a striking patterned red dress, head held in a haughty manner, it was Beaverbrook who purchased the work, preventing Rubinstein from destroying the portrait. Sutherland had produced three portraits of Rubinstein; one was destroyed by fire, one is in the Beaverbrook Art Gallery, Canada, and the other is in the National Portrait Gallery, Canberra. The portrait Beaverbrook saved was displayed at the Tate gallery in London soon after Sutherland completed the commission and was honoured with a visit by the Queen and Queen Mother. It was also the subject of a critique in the British newspapers – the publicity assisting Rubinstein to change her mind about the portrait and allow Beaverbrook to have his way.

The attention to the portrait inspired Rubinstein's arch-rival, Elizabeth Arden, to also commission a portrait. She had to match her rival in every way and wore a luxury gown to equally display her wealth and beauty. Rubinstein had worn Balenciaga; Arden wore Nina Ricci. Rubinstein had chosen Sutherland, who had previously painted Churchill and Beaverbrook (no doubt at the urging of Beaverbrook); Arden commissioned Simon Elwes, a British society painter and favourite of the royal family, whom Arden took to the Four Seasons hotel for the first sitting along with a party of supporters including Prince Aly Khan. She wanted the painting of the portrait to be a society event. Unfortunately, it appears that the project was not as successful as Arden imagined it might be. It involved lengthy sittings, a background painted brimming with furniture that stole the spotlight from an increasingly impatient Arden, and a loathsome final result. The picture was apparently never shown and has never been seen again, its destiny not too difficult to surmise.[18]

Vanity is easily reconciled as a reason for the celebrity to destroy a picture, the control of image of paramount importance. Artists will often respond in a far more complex manner. Works of protest and destruction now enter gallery collections as a sign of advocacy on the part of the artist or protester, or a means to communicate the fragmentation of identity. This is the case for a self-portrait by Scottish artist Craigie Aitchison that was bought by London's National Portrait Gallery in 2012. Aitchison slashed the work in the late 1950s–early 1960s after he had been told that he looked good in the picture – the work is a protest against the proliferation of the promotion of self in contemporary media. His exploration of identity as conveyed through the self-portrait was harmed by the standard comment – the slashings remind of self-harm and destructive behaviour.

Artists will also willingly attempt to destroy portraits – either their own or the works of others – of persons both notorious or who have slid into disrepute. An artist managed to splatter an egg on Marcus Harvey's portrait of the Moors convicted murderer, Myra Hindley, one of the more contentious works to be included in the *Sensation* exhibition at the Royal Academy of Arts in London in 1997. Another managed to kick the substantial canvas off the wall and throw red and blue ink, while another sent a rock through the Academy windows in protest but missed the target. The violence directed at the portrait (Hindley found guilty of multiple child murders) was both a substitute for the helplessness felt by the community in the expression of their anger and public concern regarding Harvey's exploitation of the murder of children.

The Hindley portrait survived, unlike Andy Warhol's portrait installation *13 Most Wanted Men*, commissioned as one of the external works to be placed on the New York State Pavilion for the 1964 World's Fair. Warhol chose thirteen police mug shots of wanted criminals; he enlarged and then collected the images into the shape of a large square, the work presenting a confronting and daring image for global visitors to America. Of course, they never got to see the work, which was painted over in silver prior to the opening of the World's Fair. Initially, Warhol took responsibility for ordering the silver covering (and the Warhol Foundation maintains copyright over photographs of the silver-painted work), although it later transpired that organisers of the Fair were responsible for destroying the work. It was New York Governor Nelson Rockefeller who ordered the covering and, effectively, censorship of the work due to self-interest and a looming election. It seems that seven of the thirteen men had Italian names, as did many of his constituents. He did not wish for them to be unduly disturbed by the subject matter. In Warhol's inimitable style, he simply repeated the series producing individual works of each portrait.[19]

There was significant concern for the integrity of Queen Elizabeth II's art collection when the accusations and convictions of sexual abuse were made against Rolf Harris. Harris painted a highly publicised portrait of the Queen in 2005 to mark her eightieth birthday. It was the focus of an episode of the BBC's *Rolf on Art* program, and later displayed in the Queen's Gallery for six months and Liverpool's Walker Gallery in 2012, but it did not enter the Queen's collection. His work was never a favourite of art critics; the most erudite Jonathan Jones from *The Guardian* recalled the unveiling of the portrait to the press:

> [It] felt like attending some grotesquely bland cultural rite conducted by a dystopian version of Britain in which the BBC and monarchy united to promote the inanities of Rolf Art.[20]

Harris' convictions resulted in some public performances he would not have been proud of. His work disappeared from websites, galleries and collections, and singer Bonnie Tyler stated that she thought his portrait of her was 'bloody awful'; Australians also began to destroy the murals he had splashed across public places courtesy of his sponsorship with Dulux paints. His portrait and public art had been painted into Australian public life since his rise to fame in the sixties and needed to be reassessed.

Harris' portrait was part of a 50-metre mural in Richmond, Victoria, of prominent Australians that included Kylie Minogue, Nick Cave and Heath Ledger along with iconic images from popular culture – Vegemite, Skippy and Melbourne's trams. Painted in 2003 on a wall of the historic Dimmeys department store, it had safely survived the rigours of random graffiti and weather until Harris' convictions resulted in some targeted damage to the portrait. However, what it could not survive was the guilt of the artist, Hayden Dewar, who had painted the mural. Following Harris' convictions, he campaigned for approval to paint over his portrait of Harris – it took two years, but permission was eventually granted in July 2017. Dewar chose an insipid musky pink colour with which to destroy the portrait of the smiling, effervescent Harris.

Dewar was in good company in painting over the portrait as a targeted personal attack. When Madonna ended her relationship with Jean-Michel Basquiat, he asked for the paintings he had given her to be returned. The two were a couple in the early eighties when she was still to emerge as a star, but he had cemented his reputation in the New York art world. Basquiat's work mines his Haitian heritage, situates his views on his society and includes self-referential motifs.

Madonna has since commented in an interview with Howard Stern that she didn't want to return the incredible body of work. Upon receipt of the pieces, Basquiat proceeded to paint over the canvases in black as a sign that the relationship was officially over. Basquiat had painted over other canvases in anger, often motivated by the excessive commercial nature of the production environment of his work. Basquiat painted few self-portraits, but there are a number of portraits that remain, indicative of his desire to mine notions of identity.

Relationships that have ended will often result in the loss of a portrait or two – the most usual victim the photo of two lovers.

Destruction and deletion of such portraits are commonplace across social media. Such destruction is easy – it is a means to banish from sight. Yet the destruction of a portrait by artist David Hockney had quite the opposite objective – the original portrait did not satisfy his memory and so he needed to start again.

Hockney could not reconcile the first rendition of his 1972 work *Portrait of an Artist (Pool with Two Figures)* – now in a private collection – with the emotion associated with his depiction of his former lover Peter Schlesinger. He worked on the picture for six months, eventually destroying it to begin again; the next version took only two weeks. In the 1974 film by Jack Hazan, *A Bigger Splash,* we are transported to Hockney in the seventies and the creative process that was the genesis for the famous portrait. He states that:

> I couldn't have done it in that time unless you'd wasted all that time on the other. The one picture that took two weeks really took six months and two weeks.

It is a portrait of a past relationship reconstructed. Hockney had to ask Schlesinger to pose for photographs so that he could redo the portrait from scratch – not a path that could be negotiated too easily.

Contemporary Irish artist Oliver Jeffers commits to a partial destruction of his portraits, part of the long tradition of anti-art. He paints a portrait, sometimes of a famous subject such as Bono, then invites visitors to his studio to witness the picture being ceremoniously dipped into a tub of paint, like a coffin being lowered into a grave. The subject sometimes assists with the destruction; the portrait's connection with the living is severed. It's an act that underlines the notion of the interchangeability of the portrait and the person: viewers often feel a deep sense of loss as the portrait is gradually destroyed. The Colombian artist Cesar Biojo works slightly differently: he paints realistic portraits of his subjects, then smears and smudges – the act of creation linked to the act of destruction, which becomes intrinsic to the work. Through the destruction of the portrait image that he has created, he mimics a human nature so eager to smear others.

Unfortunately, smearing of a portrait was the fate of the fresco portrait of Christ, *Ecce Homo* by Elías García Martínez, painted during the 1930s on the walls of the Spanish church Santuario de Misericordia. The local cleaning woman, in her efforts to preserve the work, had accidentally taken off the fine physiognomic features of Christ and, in order to restore the portrait, replaced it with a humorous childlike rendering – some relating the image to a pale-faced monkey. The portrait is effectively destroyed but has become a tourist attraction, and in the meantime the original portrait Martínez used as the basis for his fresco has been discovered in an antique shop – the media attention from the act of destruction securing the value of the work further.

Drowning in the material of the work are the wax portraits by Swiss-born artist Urs Fischer. His most recent work, *Dasha* (2018), a portrait of his friend Dasha Zhukova, was exhibited in the window of the Gagosian gallery in London. The wick was set alight for the work to slowly burn and the wax melt for the duration of the exhibition – an exhibition extended to accommodate the slow burn. The portrait became a pile of gooey pink wax, dripping and melting from a form identifiable as a portrait to another abstractly spread on the gallery floor. The public is fascinated by this transformation of reality to a state that bears no trace of the original features.

The gradual destruction of a series of portraits engraved into the sand of the beaches of Britain marked the centenary of the Armistice in 2018. The portraits were of those who had died in the war and were placed at pivotal sites throughout Britain, the features of the portraits only fully realised from a distant point of view. Ever so gradually consumed by the tide, each portrait was washed away, the work of the artist gone just as so many lives were taken too soon.

ACKNOWLEDGEMENTS

I wish to thank the staff of the following institutions for their assistance, digitisation of material and access to collections essential for the production of this book: State Library of Victoria; Monash University Library; University of Melbourne; State Library of New South Wales; National Portrait Gallery, London; New York Public Library; Metropolitan Museum of Art, New York; National Gallery of Art, Washington; White House Historical Association; Isabella Stewart Gardner Museum; Harvard Art Museums; the Churchill Archive and Dallas Museum of Art.

Thank you to Russell Burrows for supplying and granting permission for the image of the portrait of Sir Winston Churchill, and also many thanks to Adam Lowe from Factum Arte for his help in making those important connections. Thank you to Dr Robert Carrer from the Graham Sutherland estate for his permission to publish the image of the portrait of Sir Winston Churchill. Thank you also to Etienne Cohen, Paul Davis and Steven Salgo for their permission to reproduce the image of the Bondi Indigenous mural and for their work in the provision of permissions from the families of those represented in the mural. For assistance with the supply of images, I would like to thank the Gerhard Richter Studio, Bridgeman Images and Nicole Garmston.

I am indebted to Kirsten Abbott at Thames & Hudson for her hard work, wonderful assistance and expert advice on this publication. Thank you also to Jessica Levine and Vanessa Battersby for their most insightful editing of the text and guidance in relation to the structure. Daniel Watts, Thames & Hudson, has supported this publication from our very first discussions, and I am grateful for his leadership.

Thank you to the amazing community of writers who also love the exploration of the portrait. My study of portraiture all began with Leigh Astbury, and I thank him for his wonderful scholarship. I am also grateful to Professor Ronald S. Sullivan Jr from Harvard Law School, who kindly gave his time to chat about the impact of the damage to the portraits in Wasserstein Hall. Equally, thank you to the community on Mer Island for making me welcome and including me in your conversations.

My friends and family provided extraordinary support and guidance. Thank you to Jack Rush QC for reading passages and for his assistance. Thank you to Mike Whitehead for exploring the portraits with me. To my mother, Joyce Cotter, you continue to astound everyone with your support, and, of course, thank you to Shane and Andrea and families.

My children were there to greet the research every morning and help prosecute ideas and concepts. Thank you to Tess, James and Matt for making it all worthwhile.

ENDNOTES

Introduction

1 Helga Prignitz-Poda, *Hidden Frida Kahlo* (Munich: Prestel, 2017), 9.
2 Gannit Ankori, *Frida Kahlo* (London: Tate Publishing, 2005), ch. 4, 19.
3 Raymond Gill, 'Exclusive: Malcolm Turnbull as a "Fat, Greedy, C…"', *Daily Review*, 1 February 2016.

Chapter 1: Bulldog or Cherub: The Legacy of Winston Churchill

1 Lord Moran, *Winston Churchill: The Struggle for Survival 1940–1965* (London: Constable, 1966), 620.
2 Mary Soames, *Clementine Churchill* (London: Cassell, 1979), 501.
3 Malcolm Yorke, *The Spirit of Place: Nine Neo-Romantic Artists and Their Times* (London: Tauris Parkes, 2001[1988]), 141.
4 Soames, 501.
5 Frederick Woods, *Artillery of Words: The Writing of Sir Winston Churchill* (London: Leo Cooper, 1992), 40.
6 Winston Churchill, *Liberalism and the Social Problem* (London: Hodder & Stoughton, 1909), 78.
7 Winston Churchill, letter to Lady Randolph Churchill, 25 April 1898, quoted in David Lough, *No More Champagne: Churchill and His Money* (London: Head of Zeus, 2015), 51.
8 Lough, 73.
9 David Day, *Menzies & Churchill at War* (East Roseville: Simon & Schuster, 2001 [1986]), 66.
10 Kathryn Perera, 'The Labour Party or Nothing: Jennie Lee', *Labour List*, 22 November 2010.
11 Kenneth Clark, 'Introduction', in *An Exhibition of Paintings and Drawings by Graham Sutherland* (London: Arts Council of Great Britain, 1953).
12 Peter Fuller, *Images of God: The Consolations of Lost Illusions* (London: Chatto & Windus, 1985), 91.
13 James Lancaster, 'The 1954 Sutherland Portrait', *Finest Hour*, vol. 148, 2010.

14   John Hayes, *The Art of Graham Sutherland* (New York: Alpine Fine Arts Collection, 1980).
15   Clementine Churchill, meanwhile, referred to Sutherland as a 'Wow', writing to her daughter, 'He really is a most attractive man.' (Soames, 487).
16   Elsbeth Juda, 'Perspectives: Elsbeth Juda, photographer, on a life in pictures', *New Statesman*, 21 May 2009.
17   Winston Churchill, 'The Paintings of Winston Churchill', *Life*, 7 January 1946, 44.
18   Winston Churchill, 'Painting as a Pastime', *The Strand Magazine*, 1922.
19   Anthony Montague Browne, *Long Sunset: Memoirs of Winston Churchill's Last Private Secretary* (London: Cassell, 1995), 171.

Chapter 2: An Artist's Choice: Adolf Hitler

1   Kathleen Marie Higgins, 'Rebaptizing our Evil: On the Revaluation of All Values', in *A Companion to Nietzsche*, ed. Keith Ansell Pearson (West Sussex: Wiley-Blackwell, 2009), 404.
2   Frederic Spotts, *Hitler and the Power of Aesthetics* (Woodstock: Overlock Press, 2003), 11.
3   Oscar Pinkus, *The War Aims and Strategies of Adolf Hitler* (North Carolina: McFarland & Co., 2005), 481.
4   US Department of Defense, *Information Paper DAMH-MDC*, 21 November 2001.
5   Simon Schama, *Landscape and Memory* (London: Harper Collins, 1995), 119.
6   Robert Storr, *Gerhard Richter: Forty Years of Painting* (New York: Museum of Modern Art, 2002), 19.
7   Dietmar Elger, *Gerhard Richter: A Life in Painting* (Chicago: University of Chicago Press, 2002), 6. This is confirmed in conversation with Michael Kimmelman; see: 'Gerhard Richter: An Artist Beyond Isms', *The New York Times*, 27 January 2002.
8   Storr, 40.
9   Gerhard Richter, *Text* (London: Thames & Hudson, 2009), 511. This quotation is from a discussion with Jeanne Anne Nugent in 2006.
10   Darryn Ansted, *The Artwork of Gerhard Richter: Painting, Critical Theory and Cultural Transformation* (London: Routledge, 2017), 16.
11   Storr, 21.
12   John L. Curley, *A Conspiracy of Images: Andy Warhol, Gerhard Richter and the Art of the Cold War* (New Haven: Yale University Press, 2013), 89.
13   Alan Riding, *And the Show Went On* (London: Duckworth, 2011).
14   John J. Curley, 'Controlling Doubt: Abstract Painting and Photography', *Photography and Doubt* (London: Routledge, 2016), 206.
15   Richter, 13.

16 Storr, 27.
17 Banned artworks, being far more valuable, were not usually burnt but were instead offloaded by Nazi officials to private collectors to garner much-needed funds to support Hitler's armies.
18 Reprinted in Elger, 31.
19 Stefan Gronert, 'Art History as Survey', in *Gerhard Richter: Early Work, 1951–1972* (Los Angeles: J. Paul Getty Museum, 2010), 128.
20 Richter, 48.
21 Storr, 41.
22 Richard Brilliant, *Portraiture* (London: Reaktion Books, 1991), 11.

Chapter 3: Presidents and Dictators

1 Gordon Hendricks, 'The Eakins Portrait of Rutherford B. Hayes', *The American Art Journal*, vol. 1, no. 1, 1969, 104–114.
2 Henry Adams, *Eakins Revealed: The Secret Life of an American Artist* (Oxford: Oxford University Press, 2005), 410.
3 Aida D. Donald, *Lion in the White House: A Life of Theodore Roosevelt* (New York: Basic Books, 2007), 178.
4 Theodore Roosevelt, letter to Kermit Roosevelt, White House, Washington, 1 February 1903, Theodore Roosevelt Collection, MS Am 1541 (48), Harvard College Library.
5 *The San Francisco Call*, 17 May 1903.
6 'Gems of New French Salon Exhibition', *New York Tribune*, 30 April 1903.
7 'Destructive Artists: The Ruin They Wrought While Smarting Under Criticism', *San Bernardino Sun*, 10 February 1906, 25.
8 'President Taft's Eulogy for his Aide, Archibald Butt, Who Went Down with the Titanic Just Days Before', 19 April 1912, Shapell Manuscript Foundation, <www.shapell.org/manuscript/president-taft-mourns-life-lost-on-titanic>.
9 Archie Butt, *The Letters of Archie Butt* (Garden City: Doubleday, Page & Company, 1924), 329.
10 Butt, 341.
11 'To Paint the President', *The Courier* (Lincoln, Nebraska), 31 January 1903, 8.
12 'The Academy Exhibition', *Art Amateur*, vol. 24, no. 6, May 1891, 144–5.
13 Michael R. Canfield, *Theodore Roosevelt in the Field* (Chicago: University of Chicago Press, 2015), 7.
14 Canfield, 10.
15 Henry James, *Picture and Text 1893* (New York: Harper & Brothers), 115.
16 'Interesting art treasures of the White House', *Washington Times*, 6 March 1904.
17 John F. Kennedy, speech in honour of poet Robert Frost, Amherst College, Massachusetts, 26 October 1963.

18 No contemporary dictators have been female.

19 Diego Rivera, *Portrait of America* (London: George Allen & Unwin, 1935), 23.

20 Jan Plamper, *The Stalin Cult: A Study in the Alchemy of Power* (New Haven: Yale University Press, 2012), 183.

21 Richard Brilliant, *Portraiture* (London: Reaktion Books, 1991), 47.

22 Anita Pisch, *The Personality Cult of Stalin in Soviet Posters, 1929–1953* (Acton: Australian National University, 2016).

23 Kenneth Nyangani, 'Housing scheme beneficiaries ordered to hang Mugabe portraits', *NewsDay Zimbabwe*, June 2017.

24 Kenneth Nyangani, 'Register to vote or lose your stands', *NewsDay Zimbabwe*, 7 November 2017.

25 Michel Foucault, *Power/Knowledge: Selected Interviews & Other Writings 1972–1977*, ed. Colin Gordon (New York: Pantheon, 1980 [1972]), 98.

Chapter 4: Royalty and Nobility

1 Chris Bryant, *Entitled: A Critical History of the British Aristocracy* (London: Doubleday, 2017), 12–13.

2 Roy Strong, 'Holbein in England – I and II', *Burlington Magazine*, vol. 109, no. 770, 1967, 277; John Rowlands, *Holbein: The Paintings of Hans Holbein the Younger* (Boston: David R. Godine, 1985), 137–38. Both scholars note the *pentimenti*, with Rowlands considering it provides evidence for the attribution of Holbein.

3 *Revolutions de Paris*, vol. IX, 9 September 1789, 25–26, quoted in Stanley J. Idzerda, 'Iconoclasm During the French Revolution', *The American Historical Review*, vol. 60, no. 1, October 1954, 15.

4 Larry Shiner, *The Invention of Art* (Chicago: University of Chicago Press, 2001), 181.

5 Helen Weston, 'Witnessing the Revolution', in *Jacques-Louis David: New Perspectives*, ed. Dorothy Johnson (Newark: University of Delaware Press, 2006), 126.

6 *Bearded Man, Possibly Emperor Macrinus*, sculpture, early to mid-third century CE, Harvard University.

7 Eric R. Varner, *Mutilation and Transformation: Damnatio Memoriae and Roman Imperial Portraiture* (Leiden: Koninklijke Brill NV, 2004), 87.

8 Peter Dorman, 'The Destruction of Hatshepsut's Memory: The Proscription of Hatshepsut', in *Hatshepsut: From Queen to Pharaoh* (New York: Metropolitan Museum of Art, 2005), 267.

9 Dorman, 269.

10 Heather L. Sale Holian, 'The Power of Association: A Study in the Legitimization of Bianca Cappello through Medici Matriarchal Portraiture', *Renaissance Papers 2006* (Raleigh: The Southeastern Renaissance Conference, 2006), 37–39.

11 Shearer West, *Portraiture* (Oxford: Oxford University Press, 2004), 109.

12 Roy Strong, *Tudor and Jacobean Portraits*, vol. 1 (London: Her Majesty's Stationery Office, 1969), 157.

13 Rachel Scott and Annie Ablett, '"Henry and Katherine Reunited" – Conserving the Portrait of Katherine of Aragon', National Portrait Gallery, <www.npg.org.uk/research/conservation/henry-and-katherine-reunited-conserving-the-portrait-of-katherine-of-aragon>.

14 Philip Mould, 'Over-Paint Uncovered', *Lost Faces: Identity and Discovery in Tudor Royal Portraiture* (London: Philip Mould Ltd, 2007).

15 Bruce Fellman, 'Looking for Lady Jane', *Yale Alumni Magazine*, May/June 2007.

16 Elizabeth W. Pomeroy, *Reading the Portraits of Queen Elizabeth I* (Connecticut: Archon Books, 1989), 17.

17 Pomeroy, 1.

18 Pomeroy, 17.

19 'Portrait of Queen Elizabeth I (1533–1603) with a hidden serpent', National Portrait Gallery, <www.npg.org.uk/assets/files/pdf/displays/concealedandrevealed/panel1.pdf>.

20 Roy Strong, *Tudor and Jacobean Portraits*, 104.

21 Barbara J. Harris, 'Defining Themselves: English Aristocratic Women, 1450–1550', *Journal of British Studies*, vol. 49, no. 4, 2010, 734–752.

22 Pomeroy, 38.

23 Amy Blakeway, *Regency in Sixteenth-Century Scotland* (Woodbridge: Boydell Press, 2015), 154.

24 Karl Pearson, 'The Skull and Portraits of Henry Stewart, Lord Darnley, and their Bearing on the Tragedy of Mary, Queen of Scots', *Biometrika*, vol. 20B, no. 1, July 1928, 103.

25 Robert Stedall, *The Survival of the Crown: Volume II: The Return to Authority of the Scottish Crown following Mary Queen of Scots' Deposition from the Throne, 1567–1603* (Sussex: Book Guild Publishing, 2014), 237.

26 Forrest P. Chisman, 'The Portraits of Mary, Queen of Scots, "En Deuil Blanc": A Study in Copying', *The British Art Journal*, vol. 6, no. 2, 1 October 2005, 27.

27 John Guy, *'My Heart is My Own': The Life of Mary Queen of Scots* (London: Fourth Estate, 2004), 447. This miniature portrait series was given to one of her maids-in-waiting, Elizabeth Curle. See also: Roderick Graham, *The Life of Mary Queen of Scots* (New York: Pegasus Books, 2009).

28 Lionel Cust, *Notes on the Authentic Portraits of Mary, Queen of Scots* (London: J. Murray, 1903), 60.

29 Agnes Strickland, *Lives of the queens of England, from the Norman conquest: with anecdotes of their courts, now first published from official records and other authentic documents private as well as public* (Philadelphia: Blanchard and Lea, 1857), vol. VII, 34.

30 Strickland, 40.

31 Strickland, 64.

32 John Guy, *Queen of Scots: The True Life of Mary Stuart* (New York: Mariner, 2005), 489.

33 'Student Jailed for Slashing Princess Diana's Portrait', 31 August 1981, United Press International, <www.upi.com/Archives/1981/08/31/Student-jailed-for-slashing-Princess-Dianas-portrait/8665368078400>.

34 Christopher Cordess and Maja Turcan, 'Art Vandalism', *British Journal of Criminology*, vol. 33, no. 1, 1993, 95–102.

Chapter 5: Why Not Mao?

1 Daniel Southerland, 'Uncounted Millions: Mass Death in Mao's China', *The Washington Post*, 17 and 18 July 1994.

2 F. Dikotter, *Mao's Great Famine: The History of China's Most Devastating Catastrophe, 1958–62* (Bloomsbury, 2010), 88. It is understood that Mao made this comment at a meeting of party leaders at a conference in Shanghai in March 1959.

3 Annette Lemieux, *Black Mass*, 1991, latex, rhoplex, gesso and oil on canvas, 2.43 × 2.67 metres, Whitney Museum of American Art, New York.

4 Hong Yung Lee, *The Politics of the Chinese Cultural Revolution: A Case Study* (Berkeley: University of California Press, 1978), 87.

5 Stefan R. Landsberger, 'The Deification of Mao', in *China's Great Proletarian Cultural Revolution: Master Narratives and Post-Mao Counternarratives*, ed. Woei Lien Chong (Lanham: Rowman & Littlefield, 2002), 157.

6 John Hannon, 'In China, A Son Haunted by the Cultural Revolution', *Los Angeles Times*, 30 March 2013.

7 Claire Huot, *China's New Cultural Scene: A Handbook of Changes* (Durham: Duke University Press, 2000), 139.

8 Dan Shaw, 'Zhang Hongtu's Art Studio in Woodside, Queens', *The New York Times*, 6 November 2015.

9 'Nixon's Great Leap into China', *Life*, vol. 72, no. 8, 3 March 1972.

10 'Andy Warhol (1928–1987), *Mao*', Post-War and Contemporary Evening Sale, Christie's, New York, 15 May 2013, <www.christies.com/lotfinder/paintings/andy-warhol-mao-5684075-details.aspx>.

11 David Bourdon, *Warhol* (New York: Harry N. Abrams, 1989), 317.

12 'Andy Warhol (1928–1987), *Mao*', Post-War and Contemporary Art Evening Auction, Christie's, London, 28 June 2011, <www.christies.com/lotfinder/paintings/andy-warhol-mao-5459629-details.aspx>.

13 'Andy Warhol (1928–1987), *Mao*', Post-War and Contemporary Evening Sale, Christie's, New York, 15 May 2013, <www.christies.com/lotfinder/paintings/andy-warhol-mao-5684075-details.aspx>.

14 '*20 Pink Maos*: Warhol Takes on China's Potent Iconography', Phillips, 30 September 2016, <www.phillips.com/article/6118538/20-pink-maos-warhol-takes-on-chinas-potent-iconography>.

15 'The Dennis Hopper Collection', Christie's, New York, <www.christies.com/about-us/press-archive/details?PressReleaseID=4501>.

16 Charles Darwent, 'Anselm Kiefer: "The Independent wants to know if I am a Nazi!"', *Independent*, 11 October 2009, <www.independent.co.uk/arts-entertainment/art/features/anselm-kiefer-the-independent-wants-to-know-if-i-am-a-nazi-1799843.html>.

17 W.J.T. Mitchell, *Picture Theory* (Chicago: University of Chicago Press, 1994), 371.

18 Liao Yiwu, 'Interview With Yu Zhijian, One of the 'Three Hunan Hooligans' Who Defaced the Portrait of Mao Zedong Over Tiananmen Square in 1989', *China Change*, 1 June 2017, <chinachange.org/2017/06/02/interview-with-yu-zhijian-one-of-the-three-hunan-hooligans-who-defaced-the-portrait-of-mao-zedong-over-tiananmen-square-in-1989>.

19 Denise Chong, *Egg on Mao: A Story of Love, Hope and Defiance* (Toronto: Vintage Canada, 2011[2009]), 90.

20 Chong, 88.

21 Geremie Barmé, *Shades of Mao: The Posthumous Cult of the Great Leader* (New York: Routledge, 1996), 22.

22 'State Department document entitled "Themes" (June 29, 1989)', National Security Archive, <nsarchive2.gwu.edu/NSAEBB/NSAEBB16>.

23 Don DeLillo, *Mao II* (New York: Viking, 1991).

24 'Andy Warhol, *Mao*', Contemporary Art Evening Auction, Sotheby's, New York, 11 November 2015, <www.sothebys.com/en/auctions/ecatalogue/2015/contemporary-art-evening-auction-n09420/lot.11.html>.

25 'Andy Warhol (1928–1987), *Mao*', Post-War and Contemporary Art Evening Auction, Christie's, London, 28 June 2011, <www.christies.com/lotfinder/paintings/andy-warhol-mao-5459629-details.aspx>.

26 Hilton Kramer, 'Art: Warhol Show at Jewish Museum', *The New York Times*, 19 September 2011.

27 John Curley, 'Readymade disasters: the art and politics of Andy Warhol and Ai Weiwei', in *Andy Warhol/Ai Weiwei* (Melbourne: National Gallery of Victoria, 2015), 154.

28   Jennifer Doyle, 'Queer Wallpaper', in *The Art of Art History: A Critical Anthology*, 2nd edn, ed. Donald Preziosi (Oxford: Oxford University Press, 2009), 398.

29   Anchee Min, *The Cooked Seed: A Memoir* (London: Bloomsbury, 2013), 90.

Chapter 6: Whitewash: Erasing Black History in the West

1   Elliott J. Gorn, *Let the People See: the Emmett Till Story* (New York: OUP, 2018), 313.

2   Simeon Wright in interview with Abby Callard, 'Emmett Till's Casket Goes to the Smithsonian', *Smithsonian Magazine*, November 2009, <www.smithsonianmag.com/arts-culture/emmett-tills-casket-goes-to-the-smithsonian-144696940>.

3   Lorena Muñoz-Alonso, 'Dana Schutz's Painting of Emmett Till at Whitney Biennial Sparks Protest', *artnet*, 21 March 2017, <news.artnet.com/art-world/dana-schutz-painting-emmett-till-whitney-biennial-protest-897929>.

4   Lorena Muñoz-Alonso, 'Dana Schutz's Painting of Emmett Till at Whitney Biennial Sparks Protest', *artnet*, 21 March 2017, <news.artnet.com/art-world/dana-schutz-painting-emmett-till-whitney-biennial-protest-897929>.

5   Nigel Cooke, 'The Autopsy of Michael Jackson', 2013, <nigelcooke.net/essays-by-nigel-cooke/theautopsyofmichaeljackson>.

6   Marcel Proust, *Swann's Way* (Middlesex: Penguin, 1984), 20.

7   Ralph K.M. Haurwitz, 'UT Removes Confederate Statues from South Mall', *Statesman*, 20 August 2017.

8   Robert E. Lee, letter to Thomas L. Rosser, Lexington, VA, 13 December 1866, Lee Papers, University of Virginia Archives.

9   Patricia M. Bryson, 'Statement from the President-General 08-21-2017', United Daughters of the Confederacy, <www.hqudc.org>.

10   Adam Serwer, 'The Myth of the Kindly General Lee', *The Atlantic*, 4 June 2017.

11   Donald Trump (@realDonaldTrump), 'Sad to see the history…', Twitter, 17 Aug 2017, 6.07 am, <twitter.com/realDonaldTrump/status/898169407213645824>.

12   Martin Gayford, 'A Short History of Statue-toppling', *Spectator*, 9 January 2016.

13   R. Chambers, *The Book of Days: A Miscellany of Popular Antiquities* (London: W. & R. Chambers, 1832), 484.

14   Bruce Elder, *Blood on the Wattle*, 3rd edn (Sydney: New Holland, 2003), 23–25.

15   Malcolm Turnbull, 25 August 2017, Facebook, <www.facebook.com/malcolmturnbull/posts/the-vandalism-of-the-statues-of-james-cook-and-lachlan-macquarie-is-a-cowardly-c/10155761463461579>.

16   Vernon Ah Kee, *Born in this Skin* (Brisbane: Institute of Modern Art, 2009), 23.

17   '1826–1830', Kaartdijin Noongar-Noongar Knowledge, <www.noongarculture.org.au/1826-1831>.

18 'Secret Instructions to Lieutenant Cook', 30 July 1768, <www.foundingdocs.gov.au/
    resources/transcripts/nsw1_doc_1768.pdf>. The Admiralty's instructions were given
    'under our hands' by Sir Edward Hawke, Admiral Sir Piercy Brett and Lord Charles
    Spencer, and 'by Command of their Lordships' Sir Philip Stephens.

19 Alan L. Hill, 'Sharing Sweet Water: Culture and the Wise Use of Wetlands in
    Western Australia', PhD thesis, Murdoch University, October 2013, 58.

20 John Batman, letter to Thomas Anstey, 7 September 1829, cited in James Boyce,
    'Fantasy Island', in *Whitewash: On Keith Windschuttle's Fabrication of Aboriginal
    History* (Melbourne: Black Inc. Agenda, 2003), 31.

21 Joe Hinchliffe, 'In History there are Statues of Limitations', *The Age*, 27 August
    2017.

22 W.B. Spencer and F.J. Gillen, *The Native Tribes of Central Australia* (London:
    Macmillan, 1899), 12, quoted in *'My Dear Spencer': The Letters of F.J. Gillen to
    Baldwin Spencer*, eds. John Mulvaney et al. (Melbourne: Hyland House, 1997), 42.

23 Darren Curnoe, 'A 150-year conundrum: cranial robusticity and its bearing on the
    origin of Aboriginal Australians', *International Journal of Evolutionary Biology*, 2011,
    <dx.doi.org.ezproxy.slv.vic.gov.au/10.4061/2011/632484>.

24 Hans-Georg Gadamer, *Truth and Method*, trans. Joel Weinsheimer and Donald G.
    Marshall, 2nd rev. edn (London: Continuum, 2004), 142.

25 Bernard Smith, *European Vision and the South Pacific* (Melbourne: Oxford University
    Press, 1969 [1989]), 172.

26 Smith, 172–3.

27 Elisabeth Findlay, *Arcadian Quest: William Westall's Australian Sketches* (Canberra:
    National Library of Australia, 1998), 36. The pictures for the Admiralty refer to
    an 1814 publication of Flinders' voyage, for which he was asked to work up the
    sketches into paintings. Further references to Westall's journey are from this book.

28 Tom Roberts, 'Going North', *Argus*, 19 November 1892.

29 Margaret Hazzard, *Australia's Brilliant Daughter, Ellis Rowan* (Richmond:
    Greenhouse Publications, 1984), 63–4.

30 Makereta Mua, 'Ṣạunōan Ka 'Eagke Maoan (Forgotten But Not Lost): Rotuman
    Migration to the Torres Strait', MA thesis, University of the South Pacific,
    December 2007, 45.

31 Noel Loos and Eddie Koiki Mabo, *Edward Koiki Mabo: His Life and Struggle for
    Land Rights* (St Lucia: University of Queensland Press, 1996), 180–81.

32 Charlie Ward, 'An historic handful of dirt: Whitlam and the legacy of the Wave
    Hill Walk-Off', *The Conversation*, 20 August 2016.

33 Kate Bastiens, 'Wayside CEO apologises to those upset over removal of a mural at
    Bondi but promises a new artwork will be "bigger and better"', *Wentworth Courier*,
    7 December 2016.

Chapter 7: Artists Destroy and Destroyed

1   Amy Tritton, 'A Colonial Palimpsest: Benjamin Duterrau's Portrayals of Aboriginal People', BA (Honours) thesis, University of Tasmania, 2009, 29.

2   Stephen Scheding, *The National Picture* (Milsons Point: Random House, 2002).

3   Charles Baudelaire, letter to Édouard Manet, 11 May 1865, quoted in Alan Krell, *Manet and the Painters of Contemporary Life* (London: Thames & Hudson, 1996), 67.

4   Ambroise Vollard, *Renoir, an Intimate Record,* trans. Randolph T. Weaver and Harold L. Van Doren (New York: 1925), quoted in Ian Dunlop, *Degas* (London: Thames & Hudson, 1979), 37.

5   Vollard, 37.

6   Nancy Locke, *Manet and the Family Romance* (Princeton: Princeton University Press, 2003), 61.

7   Marni R. Kessler, 'Unmasking Manet's Morisot', *The Art Bulletin*, vol. 83, no. 3, September 1999, 485.

8   Patricia A. Favero et al., 'Reflectance imaging spectroscopy and synchrotron radiation X-ray fluorescence mapping used in a technical study of *The Blue Room* by Pablo Picasso', *Heritage Science,* vol. 5, no. 13, 2017.

9   Terence Maloon, 'Picasso's Anachronism', in *Picasso: The Last Decades* (Sydney: Art Gallery of New South Wales, 2002), 44.

10 Henry James, *Picture and Text 1893* (New York: Harper & Brothers, 1893), 57.

11 Helena Bonett, '"Deeds not words": Suffragettes and the Summer Exhibition', 19 June 2018, Royal Academy of Arts, <www.royalacademy.org.uk/article/deeds-not-words-suffragettes-and>.

12 Pam Roberts, 'Julia Margaret Cameron: A Triumph over Criticism', in *The Portrait in Photography* (London: Reaktion Books, 1992), 64.

13 Bryony Millan, 'Suffragette Action', National Portrait Gallery, <www.npg.org.uk/whatson/firstworldwarcentenary/explore/gallery-stories/suffragette-action>.

14 John Russell, *Francis Bacon* (New York: Oxford University Press, 1979), 86.

15 Robert Hughes, *Lucian Freud Paintings* (London: Thames & Hudson, 1987), 21.

16 'The Story of Lucian Freud's Stolen Portrait of Francis Bacon', *The Daily Telegraph*, 22 June 2001.

17 Dayla Alberge, 'Want Your Stolen Portrait Back?', *Daily Mail,* 20 May 2018.

18 Lindy Woodhead, *War Paint: Elizabeth Arden and Helena Rubinstein* (London: Virago, 2003).

19 'Return to the Scene of the Crime', *ARTnews*, April 2014, 28.

20 Jonathan Jones, 'I saw Rolf Harris' dark side when I questioned his portrait of the Queen', *The Guardian*, 3 July 2014.

INDEX